Bosham Bisque

BY THE SAME AUTHOR

Chester Chowder

Bosham Bisque

Recipes and Photographs by
JANS ONDAATJE ROLLS

This edition first published in 2009 by

Rare Books and Berry
High Street, Porlock,
Minehead, Somerset
TA24 8PU

www.rarebooksandberry.co.uk

Text, photographs and drawings © Jans Ondaatje Rolls

A CIP catalogue record for this title is
Available from the British Library

ISBN 978-0-9557119-2-3

Designed and typeset in Albertina by
Libanus Press Ltd, Marlborough

Printed and bound by
BAS Fine Art Printers, Amesbury

Cover photograph and the photographs on p.12, p.43 and p.88 by Charles Rolls
Back cover drawing by Alexandra Rolls

The Bosham map on the inner cover is reproduced from a document in the West Sussex Record Office:
Ordnance Survey 1:2500, Ref. sheet LX.12 (Sussex), 1st Edition, surveyed 1875

For Charlie
Sam, Alexa, George and Katie

There is a way to eat the tongue. The thalagoya is killed by placing it on the ground, doubling its head under the throat, and striking the nape with a clenched fist. The tongue should be sliced off and eaten as soon as possible after the animal dies. You take a plantain or banana, remove the skin and cut it lengthwise in half, place the grey tongue between two pieces of banana making a sandwich, and then swallow the thing without chewing, letting it slide down the throat whole.

MICHAEL ONDAATJE
Running in the Family

A thalagoya is a species of Asian monitor lizard

Contents

Foreword

Jans and I have known each other for a number of years, chatting on the touchline while watching our children play football and cricket at Westbourne House School.

When Jans told me she was writing a cookbook and wanted to give all the money from the sale of the books (not just the profits) to Winston's Wish, I was blown away by such warm generosity!

Bosham Bisque has been a project borne of Jans' love of family and community, and the result is an outstanding ambrosial cookbook, bursting with delicious recipes, creative photographs and amusing anecdotes. It is an extremely useful cookbook that is wonderfully imaginative and lovingly produced.

My own connection with Winston's Wish began in 2002 when a friend of mine lost her husband suddenly and she found herself coping alone with small and traumatised children. Winston's Wish was launched in West Sussex in 2006 and now helps families throughout the county, and trains and supports those involved with bereaved children.

Many thanks to Jans for working so enthusiastically and creatively to make this fundraising idea for Winston's Wish a reality.

JANET MARCH
Countess of March and Kinrara
President of Winston's Wish

Introduction

The inspiration for this cookbook came in two stages. Firstly, with my four children home for the summer holidays and innumerable meals looming ahead of me yet to prepare, I decided to keep a cooking diary. If I took an active interest in what I was cooking, I would produce more varied meals and the effort would seem less tedious. I started by asking my family to make a list of their favourite dishes and over the course of the summer months I prepared not only those meals, but many new ones as well. I recorded everything we ate, taking care to note all the ingredients, cooking times and methods of preparation. I made small notes about what we did, with whom we ate and even what was happening with the weather! The result was a very thick compilation of not only recipes, but of scattered memories and events. I edited and reorganised and this recipe book is the result of my efforts. In fact, it was no effort at all. I loved the preparation and our meals, as a result, were more varied and much improved.

Secondly, as I watched the life of a close friend slip away, I was sadly aware that his children were confused and very frightened. There are many children who have lost a mother, a father or a sibling and their hopes and dreams for the future have been shattered. I wanted to help them and the only way I could do so was to support Winston's Wish.

Winston's Wish was established to help bereaved children rebuild their lives after the loss of a parent or sibling. Their child-focussed approach provides support to the whole family by providing a range of services from hotlines to group sessions to activity weekends. They understand that grief is normal and necessary and have established a varied programme that has helped many, many children and their families face the future with renewed hope. All the proceeds of this book will go to Winston's Wish.

My parents have been enormously helpful in all aspects of the production of this book and for that I am hugely grateful. Sam, Alexa, George and Katie have also been terrific photographic assistants and Charlie, as ever, has been loving and supportive. Their love of food and insatiable appetites have been particularly inspiring. Thanks also to Billy Joel whose music I sang along to over and over again in the photographic darkroom!

JANS ONDAATJE ROLLS

January 2009

One cannot think well, love well, sleep well, if one has not dined well.

VIRGINIA WOOLF

Hors d'oeuvres

Yachtie's chicken liver pâté

This is a very simple pâté recipe that is most luxuriously served when on board a boat.

400 g chicken livers

65 ml brandy

2 tablespoons oil

3 cloves garlic, crushed and chopped

1 small onion, diced

125 g mushrooms, finely sliced

2 rashers streaky bacon

1 bay leaf

75 g butter

salt and pepper

Wash the chicken livers and remove any skin and tubes. Soak the livers in a bowl with the brandy. Heat 2 tablespoons of oil in a frying pan and cook the garlic and diced onion for 2 minutes. Add the mushrooms and cook for 4 minutes. Place in a food processor. Place the bacon in the frying pan and cook along with the livers on a high flame for 2–3 minutes. Do not allow the bacon to go crisp. Place all the ingredients, except the butter and the bay leaf, in a food processor and process until very smooth. Season with salt and pepper and mix well. Remove the pâté to a dish and cover with clarified butter and a bay leaf. Place the pot halfway into a pan of icy cold water to cool overnight. Place in the fridge to chill for 3–4 hours before serving. Serve with thin slices of toast.

Sussex asparagus wraps

'Asparagus abounds in Sussex during the summer months. In fact, British asparagus is widely accepted as being the best in the world due to the ideal growing conditions. It can be tricky to grow, however, but one can obtain it easily enough at roadside stalls or from the local farm shop. Salty Spanish ham complements sweet asparagus deliciously.'

12 asparagus spears	drizzle of olive oil
12 slices Spanish air-dried pork shoulder	freshly ground black pepper

Wash the asparagus spears and trim off the pithy ends. With a carrot peeler, peel the surface skin off the bottom, 2 inches from the end should be sufficient. Wrap the meat around the stalk, winding upwards, leaving the tip exposed. Drizzle with olive oil and place on a lightly greased baking sheet. Cook for 10–12 minutes at 220°C until the ham is crisp. Garnish with freshly ground pepper and serve hot.

Down Lodge devilled eggs

I am very lucky to have a good friend who keeps hens, so I'm rarely without fresh eggs. Fresh eggs are, however, harder to peel, and this recipe works best when the whites are intact. Leave your eggs, therefore, for a few days before preparing these very popular hors d'oeuvres.

6 eggs

3 tablespoons mayonnaise

1 teaspoon Dijon mustard

1 tablespoon finely chopped chives

¼ teaspoon salt

paprika to garnish

watercress

Lower the eggs carefully into a pot of water and bring to the boil. Reduce the heat and simmer for 7 minutes. Drain, and rinse under cold water until the eggs are cool enough to handle. Peel the eggs and cut them lengthwise in half. Remove the yolks and mix in a bowl with the mustard, mayonnaise, chives and salt. When the yolk mixture is smooth, fill the cavities of the hard-boiled eggs with the yolk paste. Serve on a bed of fresh watercress and garnish with a little paprika. Serves 12.

Skinny dip

'This dip is incredibly popular with the slimmers. Serve with plenty of sliced crudités.'

390 g marinated and grilled artichoke hearts

140 ml sour cream

1 tablespoon white wine vinegar

½ teaspoon salt

¼ teaspoon black pepper

3 tablespoons freshly chopped basil

1 tablespoon lemon juice

Purée all the ingredients together in a blender. Serve in a bowl surrounded with fresh raw vegetables.

Champignons à l'ail

'Mushrooms used to be known as the 'poor man's meat'. That is not the case today and a good recipe, such as this one, will satisfy the most sophisticated palate.'

16 medium field mushrooms

180 g butter

3 cloves garlic, chopped

salt and pepper

1 tablespoon parsley, chopped

1 tablespoon plain breadcrumbs

Melt the butter in a saucepan and add the garlic. Cook for 1 minute then add the mushrooms. Sauté gently for 5 minutes until the water has evaporated from the mushrooms. Season with salt and pepper and sprinkle the parsley and breadcrumbs over the top. Place under the grill for 2–3 minutes until the breadcrumbs turn golden brown. Serves 4.

Sunset vegetable tempura

'Present these vegetables just as the sun is going down. They are delightful!'

4 eggs	2 carrots, peeled
120 g plain flour	2 courgettes
¼ teaspoon salt	100 g broccoli spears
125 ml cold water	olive oil, for frying

To make the batter, beat the eggs and sift in the flour and salt. Add the water and whisk until the batter is smooth. Slice the carrots, courgettes and broccoli into medium sized strips. Dip the vegetables completely into the batter and allow the excess to drip off. Heat the oil in a frying pan and fry the vegetables for 10–12 minutes until golden brown. Remove to a couple of sheets of kitchen paper for a minute or two before arranging onto a serving dish.

Madagascan prawns

I brought these prawns to East Head for a picnic and my friend, Annoushka, took one look at them and called me Delia!

18 Madagascan prawns

2 tablespoons chopped coriander

¼ teaspoon salt

¼ teaspoon freshly ground black pepper

juice of 1½ limes

2 tablespoons Pukka hot pepper sauce

3 x 15 ml olive oil

Soak 6 wooden skewers in water for 20 minutes. Rinse the prawns with cold water and dry on sheets of kitchen towel. Place the coriander, salt, pepper, lime juice, Pukka sauce (or Tabasco) and olive oil into a bowl and mix well. Roll the prawns in the coriander marinade making sure that they are completely coated. Cover with cling film and leave in the marinade for at least half an hour. Place three prawns on each skewer. Cook on the barbecue or under the grill for 3–4 minutes on each side, basting continually. Eat with your fingers. Serves 6.

Dad's seared scallops

'My father has a carved hippopotamus (not life size) full of salt. He takes a generous pinch (or two) and covers his food. Here is a recipe that even he would agree requires no extra salt.'

24 large scallops, without roe
24 bacon rashers
60 ml olive oil

juice of ½ lemon
freshly ground pepper
1 lemon, cut into wedges

Soak 6 wooden skewers in water for 20 minutes. Roll up each scallop in a bacon rasher and pierce onto a skewer (4 per skewer). Combine the olive oil and lemon juice and brush liberally all over the kebabs. Grind fresh pepper over the top and place under a grill or on the barbecue for 4–5 minutes. Serve with a wedge of lemon. Serves 6.

Tracy's sushi rolls

❛We had a very good cook many years ago, Tracy, who showed me how to make sushi rolls. In fact, she gave me my first cooking lessons. ❜

720 g sushi rice
4 tablespoons Japanese rice vinegar
3 tablespoons white sugar
2 tablespoons salt

120 g very fresh raw tuna fish (sashimi)
4 sheets dried Japanese seaweed (nori)
soy sauce
wasabi

Sushi Rice

Rinse 2 cups of rice under cold running water until the liquid runs clear. Put into a pot and add 4 cups of water. Bring to the boil, cover, and reduce heat. Simmer for 10 minutes, or as per instructions on the package. The rice is ready when there is no more water left in the pot and the rice is saturated and sticky. Transfer the rice to a large plastic or wooden bowl. Cover with a damp tea towel to prevent it from drying out. Measure 4 tablespoons of Japanese rice vinegar, 3 tablespoons white sugar and 2 tablespoons salt into a small pot and heat on the stove until the sugar and salt dissolve. Do not boil. Separate the rice with a wooden spoon or spatula (shamoji) using a chopping motion. Pour the vinegar mixture over the rice and fold the rice over onto itself, being careful not to crush it. Repeat until the rice is evenly coated. Cover with a damp tea towel.

Tuna Fish

Cut the tuna fish into long thin strips. Place a sheet of nori on top of a bamboo mat and place a layer of prepared sushi rice on top of that. Place a strip of tuna fish horizontally on to the mat and roll the mat over on to itself. Press firmly while rolling and use the palm of your hand to prevent any rice escaping from the ends. Cut into one-inch pieces. Serve with soy sauce and wasabi. Makes 4 rolls.

Thai salmon parcels

6 There are so many wonderful exotic flavours available to the modern cook. Twenty years ago I experienced my first Thai curry thousands of miles away whilst travelling through South East Asia. Today, I can bring these piquant flavours to my kitchen table anytime! These parcels are succulent and delectable and are reminiscent of that richly fragrant land. 9

1 salmon steak

30 g crème fraîche

375 g puff pastry

olive oil

1 egg, beaten

30 g Thai green curry paste

Preheat the oven to 220°C. Roll the pastry out onto a floured work surface and cut into 3 inch squares. Wash the salmon steak and remove the skin and bones. Pat dry with a piece of kitchen paper. Cut the salmon into small cubes, approximately 3 cm x 3 cm and place on the pastry squares, just off centre. Drizzle a few drops of olive oil over the top of the salmon, along with half a teaspoon of Thai paste and a small dollop of crème fraîche. Paint the inside edges of the pastry with the beaten egg, fold over the top of the salmon, and complete the seal by squeezing the edges together using your fingertips. Paint a little more egg on the top of the parcels, place on a piece of parchment and bake in the oven for 15 minutes. Remove to a serving plate and serve while still warm.

Canute's rock oysters

'Canute sat on a chair on the foreshore of Bosham and ordered back the tide. He demonstrated that even kings have their limitations, for his feet got wet! The tide still rises high in Bosham, wetting not only feet, but cars as well. Oysters still abound in Chichester Harbour, but one must be careful not to eat them in the summer months.'

12 oysters	Tabasco sauce
lemon wedges	

Prise the oysters open using an oyster knife and present them in the half shell on a bed of crushed ice. Squeeze a little lemon juice and a dash or two of Tabasco over the raw oysters and eat them immediately. Alternatively, shallot vinegar can be used instead of lemon juice. Serves 1–2.

Salty pumpkin seeds

‘There is much frivolity at the Rolls household at Halloween. It is time to dress up, eat a lot of sweets and carve faces into pumpkins. Why not save the pumpkin seeds and roast them? If you're really feeling adventurous, add a dash of Ceylon curry powder. ’

seeds from 1 large pumpkin
30 g butter

1 tablespoon sunflower oil
salt, to taste

Carve a pumpkin and scoop out all the innards. Separate the seeds from the pumpkin pulp and wash under running water to remove all excess residue. Leave to dry overnight on a sheet of parchment in a warm corner of the kitchen (the top of an AGA, if you have one, is perfect). Grease a roasting tin and melt the butter in it. Add the seeds, coat with the butter and season with salt. Roast in a preheated 180°C oven for 20–25 minutes until the seeds are crisp and golden brown. Serve hot.

Gulbis' dill pickles

'When the Latvian tennis player Ernests Gulbis left behind a jar of homemade dill pickles at the home of our friends, Susie and John Wells, I got terribly excited. Susie knows that I am half Latvian and have a passion for dill pickles, and so she very kindly gave me the coveted jar. I carefully counted out each one of the ingredients and this is the recipe that I came up with. They are vinegary, crunchy, and not at all sweet – just as dill pickles should be.'

5 bay leaves	1 kg small cucumbers
3 juniper berries	2 sprigs fresh dill
5 stalks from vine	2 cloves garlic
1 medium dark green cabbage leaf, torn in half	750 ml water
3 leaves from grape vine	3 tablespoons kosher salt
6 peppercorns	6 tablespoons white vinegar

Put the bay leaves, juniper berries, vine stalks, cabbage leaf, vine leaves and peppercorns into a large pickling jar. Wash the cucumbers, trim the ends and place into the jar until it is nearly full. Top with a few sprigs of dill and the 2 garlic cloves. Combine the water, salt and vinegar and stir until the salt has dissolved. Pour over the cucumbers and screw the top on tightly. Gently shake the jar and leave it in a sunny position for 4 or 5 days to ferment. Refrigerate.

Blockbuster popcorn

'My father once wrote a song for me called "The Greatest Popcorn Maker in the World". There was a time when I used to make popcorn every night, to perfection – not one kernel left, not one piece burnt. Although I make it less frequently now, I still enjoy my favourite films with a large bowl of popcorn on my lap.'

100 g popcorn	60 g butter
1 tablespoon oil	salt, to taste

Pour the oil into a large pot and add the popcorn. Place on top of a hot hob and start shaking the pot. There is no need to cover the pot until the kernels lighten in colour and start 'dancing'. Once this happens, put the top on the pot and shake continuously until all the kernels have popped. Remove from the heat and pour into a large bowl. Melt the butter and pour over the top of the popcorn. Sprinkle some salt over the top and mix in. Eat while still warm.

Cooking is like love. It should be entered into with abandon or not at all.

HARRIET VAN HORNE
Vogue, Oct, 1956

Soups
& Sauces

Bosham beetroot soup

❛ I plant my beetroot seeds in April and by September they are absolutely enormous. It doesn't matter, because they make a delicious soup. **❜**

300 g beetroot, peeled and chopped

300 ml vegetable or chicken stock

1 medium potato, peeled and cubed

1 bay leaf

¼ teaspoon salt

150 ml sour cream

12 sprigs fresh dill, chopped

Bring the stock to the boil and add the beetroot, potato, bay leaf and salt. Cook, uncovered, until the vegetables are tender (one hour). Remove the bay leaf and liquidise the vegetables. Stir in two-thirds of the sour cream. Return to heat but do not boil. Garnish each serving with a dollop of sour cream and some fresh dill. Serves 4–6.

Summer gazpacho

'If I have some friends over for a game of tennis and a light lunch, I'll often serve this cold soup. It is refreshing and low calorie.'

5 ripe plum tomatoes

1 green pepper

1 red pepper

1 yellow pepper

1 spring onion, chopped

1 cucumber

2 cloves garlic, crushed and chopped

3 tablespoons olive oil

2 tablespoons finely chopped basil

4 tablespoons wine vinegar

salt and pepper, to taste

Place the tomatoes into a large pot of boiling water and let stand for 5 minutes. Drain. Remove the tomato skins and chop into pieces. Wash the peppers and remove the seeds. Chop into pieces. Wash the cucumber and cut into pieces as well. Put all the ingredients into a food processor or blender and combine well, but do not liquefy completely. Season with salt and pepper. Serve chilled with crispy croutons (p.63). Serves 4–6.

Fisherman's onion soup

> This dish is to be recommended when the weather is particularly cold and blustery. It will warm you right through and is one of the great comfort meals.

Soup Base:
4 onions
1 teaspoon butter
1 tablespoon oil
1½ litres chicken stock
1 teaspoon chopped parsley
salt and pepper, to taste
1 bay leaf

Topping:
½ baguette
90 g Gruyère cheese

Peel and chop the onions. Heat the oil in a large pot and melt the butter. Cook the onions until they are soft, but not brown. Pour in the chicken stock, bay leaf and chopped parsley and season with salt and pepper. Bring to the boil and leave to simmer for half an hour.

To make the topping, slice the baguette into slices and toast. Grate the Gruyère cheese and liberally cover the bread slices with the cheese. Remove the bay leaf from the pot. Ladle the soup into each bowl and cover the soup with as many pieces of bread and cheese as possible. Put a little bit more cheese into each bowl to completely cover the tops of the bowls. Place under the grill until the cheese has melted and is golden brown. Serves 4.

Chester chowder

'When I was 18, I compiled a cookbook called *Chester Chowder*. It included lots of recipes from friends, but I omitted to include an actual recipe for Chester Chowder. It is long overdue, but here it is at last.'

400 g fresh haddock

250 g scallops (with or without roe)

250 g lobster meat, cooked

120 g butter

2 cloves garlic, chopped

2 onions, finely chopped

1 tablespoon plain flour

1 litre whole milk

1 bay leaf

1 tablespoon tarragon, chopped

1 tablespoon flat-leaf parsley, chopped

salt and pepper

3 potatoes, peeled and diced

8 sprigs parsley, to garnish

1–2 teaspoons curry powder

dark rum, to taste

Rinse the haddock and scallops under cold water and pat dry. Cut the fish and lobster into 2 cm pieces. The scallops can remain whole. Melt the butter in a soup pot and cook the garlic and onions gently for 1 or 2 minutes. Add the flour and stir. Pour the milk into the pot a little at a time until it is well integrated. Add the bay leaf and herbs and season with salt and pepper. Add the potatoes to the pot and bring the broth gently back to the boil. Simmer gently for 10 minutes. Add the fish, scallops, and curry powder and cook gently for 10–15 minutes. Add the lobster meat and rum. Heat gently and serve. Garnish with parsley. Serves 8.

Chicken noodle soup with stars

‘This was my favourite soup as a child. In fact, it probably still is my favourite. It is clear and light and the noodles make it fun to eat. ’

1 tablespoon oil

1 chicken breast

1 litre chicken stock, fresh or from a cube

50 g spaghetti

50 g pasta stars

1 tablespoon parsley, very finely chopped

salt and pepper

Heat the oil in a frying pan and add the chicken breast. Cover. Reduce the heat and cook for 12 minutes on each side. Remove from heat and cut into very small pieces. Bring the chicken stock to the boil. Break the pieces of spaghetti into small pieces and put them into the boiling broth. Add the stars and cook for 7 minutes. When the pasta is nearly cooked (follow instructions on package), add the parsley, chicken and all the chicken juices. Boil for another couple of minutes until the pasta is cooked. Season with salt and freshly ground black pepper. Serves 4.

Bosham bisque

'King Harold attended mass at Bosham Church in 1064 before setting sail to meet William of Normandy. Ostensibly, he went to proclaim his loyalty to Edward, but really he went to warn William that he would claim the throne when Edward died. He did indeed become king, only to fall in 1066 to William at the Battle of Hastings. The Saxon church is still the most distinguishing landmark in Bosham. It stands stalwartly, taller than the village houses, and is a sight that will always inspire me. '

1 cooked lobster	2 x 400 g tomatoes in tomato juice
4 haddock fillets, skinned	500 ml fish stock
4 cloves garlic, chopped	1 teaspoon sugar
1 medium onion, finely chopped	1 bay leaf
1 medium carrot, thinly sliced	250 ml dry white wine
3 tablespoons olive oil	500 ml water
5 g flat-leaf parsley, chopped	salt and pepper
1 tablespoon lemon juice	1 tablespoon fresh parsley, to garnish

Heat the oil in a deep saucepan and gently fry the garlic and onion for 5 minutes. Add the carrot, parsley, bay leaf, lemon juice and wine and boil for 4 minutes. Add the tomatoes, water, sugar and fish stock and simmer for 25 minutes. Season with salt and pepper. Wash, de-bone, and dry the haddock fillets and add to the soup pot. Bring to the boil and simmer gently for 10–12 minutes. Meanwhile, extract the meat from the lobster and cut it into 2 cm pieces. Add the lobster meat and the lobster legs (still in their shells) to the bisque and mix in, stirring gently, for 1 minute. Remove from the heat and serve in bowls with a garnish of parsley on top. Serves 4.

Cucumber vichyssoise

'Every summer I participate in the annual Winston's Wish tennis tournament. It is a family round robin event in which matches are played in the morning and lunch is served afterwards. This year, I served this chilled soup, which was much appreciated!'

3 cucumbers, peeled

10 g salt

3 tablespoons crème fraîche

30 g butter

2 leeks, finely sliced

1 medium potato, peeled and diced

½ onion, diced

300 ml whole milk

salt and pepper

3 tablespoons sour cream

fresh chives

Slice the cucumber into strips and remove the seeds. Cut into thin slices and sprinkle salt over the top. Mix in. Leave for 10 minutes and then rinse under cold water. Place in a blender with the crème fraîche and liquidise. Strain through a sieve and set aside.

Melt the butter in a saucepan and gently cook the leeks, potato and onion for 15 minutes. Season with salt and pepper. Pour in the milk and bring to the boil. Reduce the heat and simmer for 25 minutes. Set aside to cool, then liquidise in a blender. Put through a strainer, using the back of a wooden spoon or spatula to push the liquid through. Combine the two mixtures in a pitcher and leave to chill in the fridge for 3 hours. Stir, then pour into shot glasses. Garnish with a few drops of sour cream and a little chopped chives. Serves a crowd.

Chunky chicken soup

'We often have this soup on a Sunday evening, using up any leftover chicken from the lunch roast. Serve with fresh bread and you have a meal.'

2 onions, diced

1 tablespoon olive oil

1 or 2 chicken carcasses

2½ litres water

8 carrots, coarsely chopped

6 stalks celery, coarsely chopped

juice of ½ lemon

¼ teaspoon salt

3 peppercorns

bouquet garni

6 tablespoons freshly chopped coriander

1 tablespoon parsley

2 boneless, skinless chicken breasts, cooked

4 tablespoons fresh coriander, chopped

Fry the onions in a saucepan for 2 minutes until soft, but not brown. Put the chicken carcass(es) into a large pot and add the water. Add six carrots, fried onions, celery, lemon juice, salt, peppercorns, bouquet garni, coriander and parsley. Bring to the boil. Reduce the heat and simmer, uncovered, for one hour. Remove from the heat and cool. Skim off as much fat as possible and, if desired, completely strain the soup. I prefer to remove the bones only as I quite like the vegetables. Chop the chicken breasts into chunky pieces and add to the broth along with two chopped carrots. Season with salt and pepper. Simmer until the carrots are soft and garnish with a little fresh coriander. Serves 6.

Maroon carrot and ginger soup

'Maroon carrots are becoming increasingly available in England. Any colour of carrot can be used in this recipe, but the maroon carrot offers an interesting variation to the common orange variety.'

2 tablespoons oil	4 maroon carrots
2 cloves garlic, diced	4 pints water
1 medium onion	1 bay leaf
1 stock cube	1 potato, coarsely chopped (optional)
2 stalks celery	sour cream
3 tablespoons ginger root, chopped	1 teaspoon coriander, chopped
¼ teaspoon ground nutmeg	salt and pepper, to taste

Wash and dice the vegetables. In a large pot, heat the oil, add the diced garlic and onion and cook for 1 minute. Crumble a stock cube into the pot and add the celery, ginger and nutmeg. Cook for three more minutes. Add the carrots, water and bay leaf to the mixture. Bring to the boil. If you like, add the potato (this makes a thicker soup, ideal for wintertime). Simmer for twenty minutes, uncovered, until the carrots and potatoes are soft when squeezed. Separate the vegetables from the broth and remove the bay leaf. Purée half the vegetables. Add half the stock and put the puréed vegetables through a strainer. Repeat for the remaining vegetables and broth. Return all the soup to a pot and reheat, but not to boiling point. Season with salt and pepper. Serve with a dollop of sour cream and garnish with fresh coriander. Serves 4.

Cheesy cheese sauce

This cheese sauce will liven up all vegetable and pasta dishes. Add a little extra cheese if you like your sauce very cheesy.

50 g butter

¼ teaspoon mustard powder

50 g flour

500 ml whole milk

250–350 g Cheddar cheese

salt, to taste

Melt the butter in a saucepan and stir in the mustard powder and flour. Reduce the heat and whisk the milk in gradually, keeping the consistency smooth. Remove from heat and stir in the cheese. Add a little salt, if necessary. Serve immediately.

Béchamel (white) sauce

This is the foundation recipe for all white sauces. It is delicious poured on top of chicken, fish or freshly cooked vegetables.

50 g butter

40 g flour

525 ml whole milk

In a saucepan, melt the butter and mix in the flour until a paste forms. Reduce the heat and add the milk little by little, stirring continuously with a wire whisk. When the milk is completely integrated remove from the heat. Cover with cling film until ready to serve. If you want a runnier sauce, add more milk or a little stock. Season to taste.

Holiday hollandaise

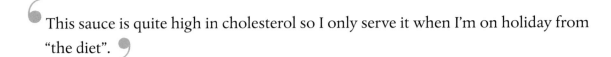

This sauce is quite high in cholesterol so I only serve it when I'm on holiday from "the diet".

250 ml white sauce (p.47)	a dash of Worcestershire sauce
3 egg yolks	1 tablespoon lemon juice
60 g butter	salt and pepper, to taste
a dash of Tabasco sauce	

Make a white sauce and cool. Whisk the egg yolks until creamy and add about 5 tablespoons of the white sauce. Mix well. Add the rest of the sauce, completely integrating the eggs. Using a double boiler, heat the sauce while adding the butter, one pat at a time. Stir continually, being careful not to cook the eggs. Add a dash of Tabasco and Worcestershire sauce. Keep stirring and add the lemon juice. Season with salt and pepper. Serve immediately.

Aioli for pasta

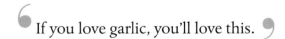

If you love garlic, you'll love this.

4–6 cloves of garlic	200–250 ml olive oil
2 egg yolks	1 tablespoon lemon juice
¼ teaspoon salt	pinch of salt and pepper

Crush the garlic cloves using a garlic press and squish them with the back of a spoon, or pestle, to make a paste. Put the egg yolks and salt into a blender. Add the garlic and mix well. Very slowly add the olive oil. Once all the oil has been incorporated, add the lemon juice. Season with salt and pepper and serve immediately.

Bullish béarnaise sauce

'A glass of red wine and a dollop of this rich sauce on top of a barbecued steak will leave you feeling bullish, even in the current economic climate. '

250 ml white sauce (p.47)

3 tablespoons white wine vinegar, room temperature

3 tablespoons white wine, room temperature

2 shallots, minced

2 teaspoons chopped tarragon

¼ teaspoon freshly ground black pepper

3 egg yolks, room temperature

60 g butter, room temperature

1 ½ teaspoons water, room temperature

salt

white pepper

Make a white sauce and allow to cool. Pour the vinegar and wine into a saucepan and add the shallots, tarragon and black pepper. Bring to the boil, reduce the heat and let simmer until the liquid has reduced by half. Whisk the egg yolks until creamy. Stir in 5 tablespoons of white sauce. Add the rest of the white sauce and stir until the egg yolks are well integrated. Stir in the tarragon liquid. Using a double boiler, return the sauce to the heat and gradually integrate the butter. Season with salt and white pepper. If the sauce curdles, stir in the water. If this doesn't work, have a whisked egg yolk on hand and blend in to the mixture. Serve immediately.

Golden rouille

'Someone once told me that saffron was worth more than its weight in gold. This may not be true by today's standards, but it has always been coveted for its seductive flavour, aroma and colour. Rouille is what makes a bouillabaisse, or chowder, absolutely fabulous.'

4 tablespoons fish broth

4 tablespoons breadcrumbs

½ teaspoon Tabasco sauce

pinch of saffron threads, crumbled

2 egg yolks

4 cloves garlic

200–250 ml olive oil

salt and freshly ground black pepper

Pour the fish broth over the breadcrumbs. Crush the garlic cloves into a paste using a mortar and pestle and stir in the breadcrumb mixture and Tabasco. Dissolve the saffron into a teaspoon of hot water. Using an electric mixer, mix the egg yolks, saffron and breadcrumb mixture together. Mix the olive oil in very slowly until it is well incorporated. Season with salt and freshly ground black pepper. This rouille will keep in the refrigerator for up to a week.

Avgolemono sauce

'This was another must-learn recipe when I married Charlie. This egg and lemon sauce renders chicken and egg dishes irresistible.'

3 egg yolks

80 ml lemon juice

250 ml hot chicken stock

Beat the egg yolks together with the lemon juice. Gradually stir in the hot chicken stock and transfer to the hob. Heat the sauce, stirring constantly, but do not boil. When sauce has thickened, it is ready.

Vampire caesar dressing

I always use lots of garlic in my salad dressing. It gives it a bit of a bite. Raw garlic also has a huge range of medicinal properties – from warding off the common cold to lowering cholesterol levels. It will even keep vampires away.

4 cloves garlic

3 – 4 anchovy fillets

2 tablespoons Dijon mustard

juice of 1 lemon

Worcestershire sauce

2 egg yolks

125 ml vegetable oil

60 g Parmesan cheese

salt and pepper

Crush 3½ garlic cloves using a mortar and pestle. Rub the inside of the salad bowl with the remaining half clove and then crush it too. Add the anchovies to the garlic and use the pestle to create a paste. Using a spoon, stir in the mustard, a pinch of salt and pepper, lemon juice, and a dash of Worcestershire sauce. Add the egg yolks and mix in an electric mixer until smooth. Slowly add the vegetable oil, mixing gently until well integrated. Stir in the Parmesan cheese and use immediately.

Breadcrumb sauce

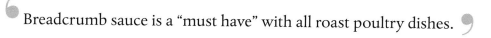

Breadcrumb sauce is a "must have" with all roast poultry dishes.

250 ml whole milk

1 medium onion, peeled

2 cloves

5 peppercorns

¼ teaspoon salt

1 bay leaf

30 g butter

50 g white breadcrumbs

salt and pepper, to taste

Add the onion, cloves, peppercorns, salt and bay leaf to the milk and heat, but do not boil. Leave on low heat for half an hour. Strain. Add the butter and breadcrumbs to the milk and bring to the boil. Stir and season with salt and pepper. Reduce heat to low and leave to simmer gently for 20 minutes. Serve warm.

Salsa verde

 This sauce is quite tangy and will liven up any grilled white fish.

2 tomatoes

3 tablespoons basil, chopped

3 tablespoons coriander, chopped

3 tablespoons flat-leaf parsley, chopped

2 garlic cloves, crushed and chopped

2 tablespoons grain mustard

1 anchovy fillet, chopped

2 tablespoons capers, drained

4 tablespoons olive oil

juice of 1 lemon

1 tablespoon fruit juice

Place the tomatoes into a bowl and cover with boiling water. Leave for 5 minutes then peel off the skin and de-seed. Cut the tomatoes into small pieces and combine with all the other ingredients. Serve with grilled fish.

Magic mayonnaise

 Homemade mayonnaise is one of those essentials that will render even a ham sandwich exciting.

2 egg yolks, room temperature

1½ teaspoons dry mustard

1 teaspoon salt

1½ tablespoons lemon juice, room temperature

a pinch of pepper

200–250 ml vegetable oil, room temperature

In an electric mixer, blend together the egg yolks, mustard, salt, lemon juice and a little pepper. On medium speed, slowly add the oil, one drop at a time, until the sauce thickens. At this point the vegetable oil can be poured in a little faster. If the sauce curdles at any point, add a previously beaten egg yolk to the mixture until the lumps disappear. Store in the refrigerator.

Ceylon dark curry powder

'Although my father left Ceylon in 1947, the pulse, the heat, the smells, the vibrancy of the island never left him and the stories he told me of that edenic island will never leave me. I visited Ceylon (now Sri Lanka) myself in 1988 and it is indeed as complex as it is beautiful. Everything is discussed, debated and argued over – even choosing the correct colour of rice is of the utmost importance. This Ceylon curry powder is full of indigenous spices. It is hot. It is aromatic – even argumentative. '

1 tablespoon basmati rice

2 tablespoons crushed red chillies

2 tablespoons coriander seeds

1 tablespoon cumin seeds

1 teaspoon fennel seeds

1 teaspoon cardamon seeds

1 teaspoon fenugreek seeds

1 teaspoon black mustard seeds

1 teaspoon turmeric

a pinch of ground cinnamon

a pinch of ground cloves

Put the rice, chillies and seeds into a dry frying pan and cook on medium heat until all the spices turn dark brown in colour. Remove from heat and leave to cool in the pan. Place the cooked spices into a spice mill or mortar and grind to a very fine powder. Add the turmeric, cloves and cinnamon and mix well. Use liberally to make strong curries and marinades.

Cumin . graines

Poivre Noir

Piment Roux

Piment Cayenne

Baies Rose

CUISINE

Piments Langues Oiseaux

Mélange

Colombo tarka dhal

"This is a slight variation of my Aunt Janet's recipe. It is thick, spicy and soupy – delicious with basmati rice or plain naan bread."

300 g red split lentils

850 ml chicken stock

2 tablespoons oil

1 teaspoon finely chopped root ginger

2¼ teaspoons ground turmeric

2 tomatoes, finely chopped

¼ teaspoon ground coriander

4 fresh green chillies

½ teaspoon salt

¼ teaspoon cumin seeds

1 teaspoon black mustard seeds

4 garlic cloves

1 red onion, chopped

10 curry leaves

10 fenugreek seeds

4 dried red chillies, whole

1 tablespoon fresh coriander, chopped

Rinse the lentils under cold running water until the water runs clear. Bring the stock to the boil and add the lentils, ginger, turmeric and ground coriander. Simmer for 30 minutes. Add more water, if necessary. Stir in the tomatoes, green chillies and salt. Heat the oil in a frying pan and gently fry the mustard seeds until they begin to 'pop'. Add the cumin seeds, garlic and chopped onion and cook for 4–5 minutes. Stir in the curry leaves, fenugreek and red chillies and cook for another 5 minutes. Combine the lentils (dhal) with the spicy oil (tarka) and mix well. Season with salt and pepper. Garnish with fresh coriander.

Breakfast is the only meal at which it is perfectly good manners to read the paper.

AMY VANDERBILT

Amy Vanderbilt's Complete Book of Etiquette

Breads
& Breakfasts

Wakey wakey white bread

'My life has changed since I invested in a bread machine. This recipe takes less than three minutes to prepare! When I set the timer and the bread is ready first thing in the morning, even my teenagers will crawl out of bed for a fresh slice.'

1¼ teaspoons yeast (for bread machines)
500 g strong white flour
1¼ teaspoons salt
1 teaspoon butter

1 teaspoon caster sugar
1 tablespoon dried milk powder
350 ml water

In a clean bread pan (it is essential that it is bone dry) add the yeast, flour, salt, butter, sugar, milk powder and water, in that order. Place the pan back into the machine and select the BASIC/WHITE setting and set the timer. 4 hours is the minimum cooking time. When the beeper sounds, remove the bread from the pan and set on a wire rack. Serve warm.

Meisner's Island soda bread

Meisner's Island in Nova Scotia is one of my favourite places on earth. It's rugged, natural and wholesome – like this bread.

300 g flour	50 g wheat bran
70 g coarse oats	2½ teaspoons soda powder
70 g cornmeal	1 teaspoon salt
50 g large oats	200 ml buttermilk
50 g wheat germ	250–300 ml water

Mix the dry ingredients together in a large bowl. Whisk the buttermilk and water together in a separate bowl and then mix in the dry ingredients. Knead into a ball and shape into a round loaf. Sprinkle a baking sheet with a little cornmeal to prevent sticking, and place the loaf on top. Shape by pressing down gently and making wheel-like incisions on top. Bake at 200°C for 20 minutes, reducing the heat to 180°C for a further 30–40 minutes. You can test to see if it is ready by putting a knife in the centre. If it comes out clean, it is ready. Place on a wire rack to cool.

Ginny's whole wheat bread

This is my mother-in-law's recipe. She is a talented woman who uses her artist's hands to sculpt each loaf. This bread is delicious on its own, or it can be served with an omelette or a bowl of homemade soup to make a wholesome light meal.

750 g whole-wheat flour	2 packets quick rising dried yeast
2 tablespoons sesame seeds	1 dessertspoon olive oil
2 tablespoons sunflower seeds	800 ml water, tepid
1 dessertspoon salt	

Mix the dry ingredients together. Mix the water with the olive oil and stir into the dry mixture. Keep stirring until the dough leaves the sides of the bowl clean. Break the dough in half. Grease and flour two bread tins and put a ball of dough into each. Sprinkle extra sunflower seeds on top and pat down. Leave in a warm place to rise. Bake at 190°C for 40 to 45 minutes.

Hearty brown loaf bread

'This is a variation of Ginny's recipe. I have adapted it for a bread machine and have made a few other changes. It is rich in omega 3 oils and is the first thing I eat each morning.'

1 ¼ teaspoons yeast

500 g seeded brown flour

1 tablespoon salt

¾ tablespoon sugar

150 g sunflower seeds

100 g pumpkin seeds

2 tablespoons sesame seeds

90 g coarse oatmeal or porridge oats

2 tablespoons bran

2 tablespoons wheat germ

125 ml olive oil

450 ml water

In a bread pan (it must be completely dry) add the yeast. Measure the flour and add it to the pan too. Add all the other dry ingredients, or any other seeds or whole grains of your choice, but do not exceed 900 g on the measuring scales. Pour in the olive oil and the water and return the pan to the bread machine. Cook on the BASIC/BAKE setting for 4 hours. When the bread is ready, remove from the pan and cool on a wire rack.

Latvian piragi

'My grandmother used to make piragi for us every time we visited. It is a Latvian custom to serve them at just about every social occasion. They are delicious any time of day, warm or cold.'

Dough
1 teaspoon yeast
500 g strong white bread flour
75 g butter
1 teaspoon salt
250 ml milk

Filling
30 g butter
325 g smoked bacon, cut into pieces
75 g chopped onions

Basting
1 egg, beaten
4 tablespoons water

Place the yeast, flour, butter, salt and milk into a bread machine, in that order. Press the DOUGH setting and press start. When the program has finished (45 minutes) remove the dough from the machine and knead it on a lightly floured surface until the dough is smooth and elastic. Divide the dough into 16 pieces. To make the filling, melt the butter in a frying pan and cook the onions on a gentle heat until they are soft, but not brown. Add the bacon and cook through, but do not crisp. Press each piece of dough with the palms of your hand until it is quite flat. Place a heaping tablespoon of the filling into the centre and fold over, sealing the edges together with your thumb and forefinger. When all the piragi have been filled and sealed place them on a sheet of parchment paper with the sealed edge on the bottom. Cover with cling film and leave them to rise (roughly 15 minutes). Beat the egg together with the water and brush over the tops of the piragi using a basting brush. Place in a preheated 210°C oven for 10 minutes or until golden brown.

Glenthorne scones

"Teatime at Glenthorne, my parents' house in North Devon, can be decadent. Fresh scones with clotted cream and jam are one of life's greatest indulgences."

200 g self-raising flour
¼ teaspoon salt
50 g butter

125 ml buttermilk
1 egg, beaten

Preheat the oven to 220°C. Sift the flour and salt together and rub in the butter. Slowly add the buttermilk. When a nice ball of dough is formed, move to a cool, floured work surface and lightly roll out the dough to 2 cm thickness. Cut out rounds using a cookie cutter (the top of a mug will do). Place on a lightly greased baking tray and paint a little beaten egg on the top of each, to glaze. Bake for 11–13 minutes or until golden brown. Makes 6–8 scones.

Crispy croutons

"There is no better way to dress up a salad than with these garlicky croutons."

⅓ loaf ciabatta bread, one day old
4 tablespoons olive oil
1 garlic clove, crushed and chopped

salt, to taste
1 tablespoon fresh basil, chopped
30 g butter

Chop the ciabatta bread into 2 cm pieces. Heat the oil and butter in a frying pan and add the garlic and bread pieces. Add the salt and chopped basil. Cook on medium heat until the croutons are brown all over. Remove from heat and leave to cool on a couple of sheets of kitchen roll. Serve on top of a soup or salad.

King Harold's French toast

'My children love this French toast on Sunday mornings. Be sure to drizzle with lots of maple syrup.'

2 eggs

3 tablespoons milk

pinch of salt

2 slices white bread

1 tablespoon oil

butter

Canadian maple syrup

Using a fork, mix together the eggs, milk and salt in a bowl. Dip each piece of bread into the egg mixture, covering both sides completely. In a frying pan, on medium heat, heat the oil and melt a little butter. Put the bread into the pan and cook until the underside is golden brown. Flip the bread over and cook the remaining side. Remove to a breakfast plate and drench with maple syrup. Eat immediately.

Middlebury blueberry bran muffins

'I had two muffins every morning for breakfast when I was at university in Vermont. The wholesome ingredients of this recipe provide an ideal start to active days and wild nights!'

400 g plain white flour

1 teaspoon salt

200 g wheat bran

200 g butter

240 g brown sugar

2 eggs, well beaten

1 tablespoon vanilla essence

1 tablespoon molasses

2 teaspoons baking soda

150 ml water

450 ml buttermilk

300 g fresh blueberries

Sift together the flour and salt and stir in the wheat bran. In an electric mixer, cream together the butter, sugar, eggs, vanilla and molasses. Bring the kettle to the boil and measure out 150 ml water and stir in the baking soda. Add the buttermilk to the water/soda mixture and stir until integrated. Add the dry ingredients to the egg mixture and gradually pour in the buttermilk mixture. Do not over mix. Fold in the blueberries. Transfer to two well greased muffin tins. Cook in a 200°C preheated oven for 20–25 minutes. Makes two dozen.

Creek House breakfast greens

My husband and I have a glass of greens every morning with our breakfast. Whenever we are feeling a little run down, we have another glass! Touch wood, we manage to ward off most colds.

2 heaping tablespoons Synergy Plus
(available from good health food stores)
1 banana

300 ml apple juice
200 ml water
3 pieces of ice

Place the juice, ice, water and banana in a blender. Add the Synergy Plus and liquefy for 15–20 seconds until the banana and ice are well integrated. Pour into two highball glasses and serve immediately.

Crispy blueberry pancakes

These pancakes are just the thing to serve when there is a crowd of ravenous children around at breakfast time. The blueberries are a delicious addition that my son, Sam, contributed to the mixing bowl one morning and they have remained an essential ingredient ever since. Be sure to drench the pancakes with lots of maple syrup before eating.

350 g strong white flour
¼ teaspoon salt
4 eggs
700 ml milk

120 g butter
1 teaspoon vanilla extract
250 g blueberries

Sift the flour and salt together into a bowl. Whisk the eggs until light and fluffy and blend into the flour. Pour the milk and vanilla into the mixture and whisk until all lumps disappear. Melt 90 g butter and stir into the batter. Fold in the blueberries. Heat a frying pan and melt a little butter into it, just enough to coat the pan. Pour enough mixture into the pan to cover the bottom. Cook for 3 minutes on each side until the pancake is crispy and golden brown. Repeat the procedure until all the batter has been used up. Serve warm with maple syrup.

Mum's crunchy granola

'I used to have a bowl of this homemade granola every morning for breakfast when I was growing up. It is delicious with milk or yoghurt and brown sugar sprinkled over the top. '

750 g oats	2 tablespoons sesame seeds
125 ml sunflower oil	6 tablespoons sunflower seeds
190 ml molasses	100 g raisins
roasted almonds, chopped	100 g chopped apricots

Preheat oven to 200°C. Measure the oil and molasses and pour into a saucepan. Heat until the oil and molasses are well integrated and the mixture is boiling gently. Remove from heat and add the oats and seeds. Transfer to a greased roasting tin and compress the mixture down hard with your hands. Place in the oven and cook for twenty minutes or until crispy and golden brown. Leave to cool in the roasting tin and add raisins, almonds and apricots before transferring to an airtight container.

Croque monsieur

'If you are in a hurry, this is a quick and easy meal. Children love it, so be prepared to make seconds.'

12 slices white bread
butter

12 slices ham
12 slices Gruyère cheese

Preheat the oven to 190°C. Butter one side of each slice of bread. Place a slice of ham and a slice of Gruyère cheese on half the slices. Close the sandwiches with the remaining slices of bread. Butter the tops of the sandwiches and place on a buttered baking tray. Do not overlap the sandwiches. Place in the oven for 8–10 minutes. Alternatively, you can fry the sandwiches. Serve with ketchup. Serves 6.

Jam yoghurts

'It is so easy to make fresh yoghurt at home. Add any flavoured preserve, or eat it plain. I often substitute fresh berries for the preserve and cover the yoghurt with a generous spoonful of honey.'

1 litre whole milk
2 tablespoons fresh plain yoghurt
2 tablespoons strawberry jam

2 tablespoons peach jam
2 tablespoons raspberry jam

Heat the milk in a pot and bring to the boil. Leave simmering for 30 minutes and remove from the heat. Remove the film of skin floating on top of the milk. When the milk reaches 49°C stir in the fresh yoghurt. Pour the mixture into 6 heat resistant glasses and cover with a layer of cling film. Put the glasses in a warm corner of the kitchen (the airing cupboard or on top of the AGA are ideal) and leave to set for approximately 9 hours. Remove the cling film and place one tablespoon of jam over the yoghurt in each glass. Cover with cling film and place the glasses in the fridge to chill. This yoghurt will keep for 5 days.

Plymouth Gin marmalade

'The botanicals in the gin marry well with the bitter flavour of the Seville oranges and make this the most delicious marmalade. '

1 kg Seville oranges, just ripe
5 tablespoons lemon juice
2 kg preserving sugar

200 ml Plymouth Gin
1.3 litres water

Put the fruit, water and gin into a casserole dish and cover. Put in a 140°C preheated oven and simmer for 4¼ hours. Skim the scum off the surface of the liquid using a perforated spoon. Take the oranges out of the pot, cut in half and remove the pips. Return the pips to the pot and simmer on the hob for 10 minutes. Put through a strainer and collect the liquid in a saucepan. Peel the skin off the oranges and slice into small strips. Add the orange flesh, the peel, the strained liquid and the lemon juice to the saucepan and bring to the boil. Remove from heat and gradually stir in the sugar. When the sugar is fully integrated, return the saucepan to the heat and boil vigorously for 15 minutes. Skim all remaining scum off the surface. While still hot, pour into jam jars and cover.

If you are ever at a loss to support a flaging conversation, introduce the subject of eating.

LEIGH HUNT
Table-Talk

Meats

Casual chicken casserole

'This casserole is perfect for a casual kitchen dinner party. It can be prepared ahead of time and reheated at the last minute. '

10 pieces of chicken

1 tablespoon oil

4 slices back bacon

1 clove garlic

½ onion

1 tablespoon chopped tarragon

4 leeks, sliced

4 carrots, sliced

1 litre chicken stock

500 g basmati rice

250 g Parmesan cheese, grated

salt and pepper

Heat the oil in a frying pan and brown the chicken pieces all over. Remove from the pan and set aside on a plate. Next fry the bacon. Cut off the fat and cut into small pieces. Add to the chicken plate. Chop the garlic and onion and fry it with the chopped tarragon. Put the leeks and carrots in the pan. Cover and cook for 10 minutes. Wash the rice and put into a greased casserole dish. Lay the pieces of chicken and bacon on top together with the partially cooked vegetables. Bring the stock to the boil and pour over the chicken and vegetables. Season with salt and pepper. Cover and place on the middle shelf of a preheated 200°C oven. Cook for 20 minutes. Remove from the oven and spread grated Parmesan cheese over the top of the casserole. Return to the oven for a further 10 minutes until the cheese is melted and golden brown. Serves 8–10.

Coq au vin

This is a great dinner party recipe and tastes better if prepared a day in advance. I love stewed vegetables so I add lots.

5 chicken breasts

5 chicken legs

3 tablespoons oil

4 pieces back bacon

2 cloves garlic, diced

15 shallots, skinned

7 carrots, roughly cut

3 stalks celery, diced

2 litres chicken stock

600 ml red wine (preferably the same one you will be having with the meal)

6 peppercorns

3 bay leaves

2 tablespoons fresh thyme

bouquet garni

400 g button mushrooms

salt

In a large oven proof pot (I use a Le Creuset pot) heat 3 tablespoons of oil and add the pieces of chicken, browning all sides. Remove from the pot and set aside. Add the back bacon and cook for 2 minutes on either side. Cut into pieces using a pair of kitchen scissors and throw away the fat. Add the garlic and shallots and fry until they are soft and just brown. Add the carrots, celery pieces and a pinch of salt. Pour in the stock and the wine and return the chicken pieces to the pot. The liquid should cover the meat, just. Add the peppercorns, bay leaves, thyme, bouquet garni and mushrooms to the pot and bring to the boil. Simmer for an hour. Cool and leave in the fridge overnight. Skim the fat off with a large spoon and reheat before serving. Serve with rice and peas. Serves 10.

Garlic thyme chicken roast with Avgolemono sauce

I always rub my chicken all over with a cut of fresh lemon prior to cooking. This not only cleans the meat, but helps to tenderise it too. This simple dish is best served on a bed of rice and can be eaten hot or cold.

4 chicken breasts	2 tablespoons olive oil
4 chicken thighs	1 lemon, sliced
1 wedge of lemon	¼ teaspoon salt
4 cloves garlic, chopped	ground pepper
8 sprigs fresh thyme	Avgolemono sauce (p.50)

Preheat the oven to 200°C. Rub the chicken pieces with a wedge of lemon. Mix the olive oil, garlic, salt, pepper, thyme and lemon slices together in a bowl. Roll the chicken pieces in the mixture and place in an ovenproof dish. Arrange the lemons, garlic and thyme on top of the chicken pieces and cover with foil. Put on the middle shelf of the oven and cook for 40 minutes. Remove the foil and return the chicken to the oven for 15 more minutes. Remove the chicken from the casserole and season with salt and pepper. Use the (strained) chicken juices to make an Avgolemono sauce. Serves 8.

Tuesday's chicken casserole

'Chicken is safe to serve insofar as it is easily digestible and is liked by everyone. A good cook has a different chicken recipe for each day of the week. These recipes, of course, can be eaten on any day.'

1.5–2 kg chicken

125 ml apricot jam

2 tablespoons Dijon mustard

2 tablespoons soy sauce

1 teaspoon Worcestershire sauce

½ teaspoon Tabasco sauce

1 clove garlic, minced

1 teaspoon fresh ginger, minced

1 onion, sliced

Preheat oven to 190°C. Wash the chicken under cold water and cut it into 6 pieces. Pat dry. Place skin side up in a greased casserole dish, or on a sheet of parchment paper. Combine the rest of the ingredients (but not the onion) in a saucepan and simmer for 2–3 minutes. Brush this glaze over the chicken and cover with sliced onions. Bake for 40–50 minutes, basting occasionally. Use the juices as a gravy. Serves 4–6.

Chicken pie for George

❝This is my son George's favourite meal.❞

800 g chicken breast meat, de-boned
1 tablespoon olive oil
½ medium onion, chopped
1 clove garlic, chopped
1 tablespoon chopped thyme

1 carrot, diced
525 ml Béchamel sauce (p.47)
salt and pepper
375 g puff pastry
1 egg, beaten

Heat the oil in a frying pan and gently fry the chicken for 15 minutes. Remove from heat and cut into 2 cm bite-sized pieces. Add the onion, garlic and thyme to the pan and cook until soft, but not brown. Add the carrot and cook for 2–3 minutes until the carrot begins to soften. Butter a pie dish and add the chicken, carrot and thyme mixture. Season with salt and pepper. Pour the Béchamel sauce over the top.

Roll out the pastry and cover the top of the dish entirely. Brush the pastry with some of the beaten egg mixture and place in the centre of a 190°C oven for 15–20 minutes until the pastry is fluffy and golden brown. Serve with a green salad. Serves 6.

Cac Robin's chicken supper

'When my son Sam was four years old, he asked me to tell him the story of Cac Robin. Sadly, I didn't know the story behind the dilapidated fishing boat P 109 so I made up a story that has fortunately been forgotten. The name "Cac Robin", however, has lasted, and is what we call the lovely old wreck that has retired on the sleepy shores of Bosham. I often serve this recipe when the children have a friend over. They all seem to love it and it can be prepared ahead of time and cooked at the last minute. Spaghetti and peas are my usual accompaniments.'

6 chicken breasts	4 tablespoons white flour
1 tablespoon chopped tarragon	2 eggs
4 cloves garlic	250 g breadcrumbs
juice of 1 lemon	4 tablespoons olive oil
500 g butter	salt and pepper

Preheat the oven to 200°C. Chop the tarragon and garlic cloves and mix with the lemon juice, butter and a little salt and pepper in a bowl. Slice each chicken breast until a neat pocket has formed, but not in half. Stuff the breasts with the flavoured butter mixture and set aside. Place the flour on a plate and season it with a pinch of salt and pepper. Whisk the eggs in a medium sized bowl. Place the breadcrumbs onto a large shallow plate and proceed to dip the chicken into the flour, then the beaten egg and then into the breadcrumbs, making sure to cover the meat entirely. Cover and store in the fridge. When ready to cook, heat the oil in a large frying pan and carefully place the breaded chicken into the pan. Fry both sides until lightly browned and place in the oven to cook for a further 15–20 minutes. Serves 6.

Smuggler's roast duck

'Duck is such a fatty bird that it is imperative that the fat be allowed to run off in the cooking process. We eat wild birds that are less fatty than the commercially reared birds, but it is still essential to prick the skin prior to cooking.'

2 large wild ducks	140 ml soy sauce
70 ml sesame seed oil	2 tablespoons ginger, chopped

Preheat the oven to 190°C. Wash the ducks inside and out and pat dry. Prick all over with a fork. Mix together the sesame oil, soy sauce and ginger. Rub the sauce all over the birds. Place the ducks breast side up on a rack in the oven for one hour. Remove from the oven and flip the birds over. Return to the oven and cook for another hour. Remove the birds again from the oven and pour some more soy sauce mixture over. Turn the oven temperature up to 200°C. Return to the oven and cook for one more hour. Serve with redcurrant jelly and breadcrumb sauce (p.51). Serves 6.

Chargrilled loin of lamb

‘We sometimes go camping when the weather is fine and instead of having a rough meal around the campfire, I like to have something that's easy, but a little special. Partially cooking a roast, such as this one, and finishing it in foil, over the coals, adds a sophisticated dimension to old-fashioned camping. ’

2.5 – 3 kg loin of lamb	250 ml olive oil
2 cloves garlic	¼ teaspoon salt
3 tablespoons thyme, chopped	¼ teaspoon pepper

Wash the loin of lamb under cold running water and set aside. Crush the garlic using a garlic press and put it in a bowl large enough to hold the meat. Add the thyme, olive oil, salt and pepper. Mix with a fork and roll the lamb in the marinade. Cover, and leave in the marinade for at least 3 hours in the fridge, turning every once in a while. Preheat the oven to 190°C. Transfer the meat to the oven and bake for one hour.

If you are camping, first cook the lamb in the oven for forty minutes and then wrap it in foil. Bring the lamb to your campsite. Once you have made a fire and the coals are red hot, place the foil-covered roast directly onto the hot coals and cook for twenty minutes. Remove the meat from the fire and carefully remove the foil whilst retaining all of the cooking juices. Place a grill over the coals and place the meat on top of the grill, searing the outside of the lamb. This should take 5 minutes. Remove from the heat and allow the meat to rest for 5 minutes before carving. Use the retained juices as gravy. Serves 8.

Aunt Janet's chicken curry

'This is an authentic Ceylon curry. The flavour intensifies if it is made a day in advance, which I recommend. If you really want to set your mouth on fire, try it with green chilli pickle and some hot chilli powder ... and keep a jug of cold water on hand!'

4 cloves	½ onion, chopped
1 onion, quartered	4 tablespoons flour
1 large roasting chicken	a pinch of saffron
3 peppercorns	1 dessertspoon Ceylon dark curry powder (p.53)
1 bay leaf	150 ml coconut milk
2 carrots, coarsely cut	¼ teaspoon salt
3 tablespoons parsley, chopped	freshly ground pepper
½ teaspoon salt	5 tablespoons chopped coriander
30 g butter	

Stick the cloves into the onion and put it into a large pot with the chicken, peppercorns, bay leaf, carrots, parsley and salt. Cover with water and bring to the boil. Reduce the heat and simmer for one hour. Remove the chicken from the stock and run the stock through a strainer. Cool 600 ml of the stock and once chilled, remove the fat. Separate the chicken flesh from the bones, dispose of the skin and chop the meat into large pieces. Put the meat on a plate and keep to one side. To make the sauce, melt the butter in a frying pan and gently fry the chopped onion with the curry powder until soft. Add the saffron and flour and mix well. Add the stock and the chicken and simmer gently on top of the stove for 10 minutes. Stir in the coconut milk and reheat but do not boil. Season with salt and freshly ground pepper. Serve with boiled basmati rice and garnish with fresh coriander.

Marmalade glazed leg of lamb

'This festive recipe is ideal for a small summer gathering. Ask your butcher to butterfly the leg of lamb for you, as it can be a bit tricky. '

1.5 to 2 kg butterflied leg of lamb
1 tablespoon vegetable oil

Glaze

125 ml marmalade

1 tablespoon minced fresh ginger

60 ml Dijon mustard

2 tablespoons soy sauce (dark)

1 teaspoon Worcestershire sauce

½ teaspoon Tabasco

Prepare the barbecue. Wash the lamb, pat dry and lay flat. Remove the excess fat and brush with oil. Combine the glaze ingredients and heat in a small saucepan. Paint the lamb with the glaze and cook for 15 minutes on the barbecue, for rare, 20 minutes for medium, and 25 minutes for well done. Brush the lamb occasionally with the remaining glaze while it is cooking. Remove from the barbecue and rest for 5–10 minutes, and then slice thinly. Serves 6.

Summer dressed lamb stew

‘It rained so much this summer that I began to prepare winter dishes and dress them up in summer attire. A dollop of Greek yoghurt and a teaspoon of freshly chopped parsley on top did the trick. ’

2 kg fillet of lamb

2 tablespoons olive oil

1 clove garlic, chopped

10 shallots, skinned

7 carrots, roughly cut

200 g button mushrooms

1½ tablespoons thyme, chopped

450 g potatoes

1 litre lamb stock

2 tablespoons parsley, chopped

salt and pepper

Wash the lamb fillet and cut into 2 cm pieces. Braise the pieces in olive oil. Remove from the pan and fry the garlic, shallots, carrots, mushrooms and thyme for 3 minutes. Put the lamb into a large casserole dish and add the vegetables. Season with salt and pepper. Slice the potatoes and create a neat top layer. Pour in the lamb stock. Cover with foil and place in a preheated 175°C oven for 2 hours. Remove the foil and turn the heat up to 200°C and cook for half an hour or until the potatoes are browned. Garnish with fresh parsley. Serves 8.

Barbarossa osso bucco

After an exhilarating day sailing around Chichester Harbour, this is a hearty meal to come back to. No matter how windswept or chilled, it always warms the old bones!

2 tablespoons oil
6 veal shanks
4 tablespoons butter
2 cloves garlic, chopped
1 onion, chopped
3 carrots, roughly cut
2 stalks celery, roughly cut
400 g tomatoes
2 tablespoons tomato purée
300 ml beef stock
365 ml Pinot Grigio wine
salt and pepper

Garnish
2 tablespoons basil, finely chopped
2 tablespoons oregano, finely chopped
2 tablespoons parsley, finely chopped
rind of 1 lemon, grated

Heat the oil in a large ovenproof casserole and brown the veal shanks on all sides. Remove from the pot, add the butter, garlic and onion and cook until soft and brown. Add the carrots and celery and cook over moderate heat for 2–3 minutes. Pour in the tomatoes, tomato purée, beef stock and wine and stir until well integrated. Season with salt and pepper. Return the veal shanks to the pot and sink them so that they are well covered in liquid. Cover the casserole and place in a preheated 180°C oven for 90 minutes. Remove the pot from the oven and simmer over medium heat, uncovered, for 30 minutes. Prepare the garnish by mixing together the basil, oregano, parsley and lemon rind. Garnish the osso bucco and serve with rice.

Wellesley's beef Wellingtons

'It is said that Beef Wellington is named after Arthur Wellesley, the first Duke of Wellington. Rumour has it that he ate beef with mushrooms and drank a tall glass of Madeira after defeating Napoleon at Waterloo in 1815.'

6 x 175 g fillet steaks

2 tablespoons olive oil

60 g butter

2 large onions, sliced

1 clove garlic, chopped

150 g mushrooms, sliced

3 tablespoons marjoram, chopped

30 ml Madeira wine

salt and pepper

2 x 400 g puff pastry

1 egg, beaten

Heat the oil in a frying pan and sear both sides of the steaks. Remove to a plate. Melt the butter and cook the onions and garlic for 1 minute. Add the mushrooms, cover, and cook until the mushrooms begin to soften (about 2 minutes). Remove the lid from the pan and stir in the chopped marjoram and any juices that may have escaped from the meat. Pour in the Madeira and simmer on top of the stove for 2 more minutes. Season with salt and pepper.

On a large floured work surface, roll out the pastry sheets and lay one on top of the other. You want to make sure the bottom sheet is well floured, to prevent sticking. Put the steaks on top of the double layer of pastry, leaving 4 cm between each fillet. Cut a shape in the pastry layers around each steak and transfer one pastry layer and its corresponding fillet to a well-greased casserole dish. Paint the exposed pastry around each steak with some of the beaten egg. Place a few tablespoons of the mushroom sauce on top of each fillet. Paint the uncovered pastry shapes with the egg and place on top of its corresponding fillet. Seal the pastry around each piece of meat by pressing the top and bottom layers together with your fingers. Place in a preheated 200°C oven for 15–20 minutes. Serve with horseradish and hot English mustard.

'Sir' loin kebabs

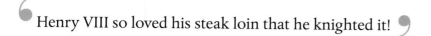

Henry VIII so loved his steak loin that he knighted it!

Kebabs	Marinade
9 sirloin steaks	120 ml olive oil
2 red peppers	40 ml balsamic vinegar
2 green peppers	4 tablespoons soy sauce
2 yellow peppers	1 clove garlic, minced
5 onions, peeled, quartered and separated	1 tablespoon fresh thyme
	2 tablespoons Dijon mustard
	¼ teaspoon ground pepper

Soak 10–12 wooden skewers in water for 20 minutes. Wash the meat under cold water and pat dry. Cut off the fat and cut into 2½ cm cubes. Wash, de-seed and cut the peppers into 2½ cm cubes. Alternate putting the meat, peppers and onion onto the skewers. To make the marinade, mix all the ingredients together in a bowl. Cover the kebabs entirely with the marinade making sure all surfaces are coated. Cover, and leave to marinate for at least three hours. Cook for 10 minutes on the barbecue or under a grill, turning occasionally. Serve with basmati rice and a green salad. Serves 10–12.

Barbecued roast beef with wild mushrooms

'My mother and I are great mushroom hunters. In the autumn we sometimes find the *Boletus* edulus, or cep. There is huge excitement all around when we do. '

Roast	Gravy
1 large rump of beef	2 tablespoons oil
1 tablespoon olive oil	1 clove garlic, crushed
freshly ground pepper	¼ onion, chopped
	350 g wild mushrooms, cleaned and sliced
	2 tablespoons flat-leaf parsley, chopped
	350 ml crème fraîche
	cooking juices from the beef
	salt and pepper

Preheat the oven to 190°C. Wash the rump of beef under cold water and pat dry. Rub olive oil all over the meat and grind black pepper over the top. Place on a rack with a tray underneath to collect the juices. Cook for 40 minutes.

Heat the oil in a frying pan and add the garlic and onion. Add the wild mushrooms and parsley and cover. Simmer for 5 minutes. Stir in the crème fraîche and simmer, uncovered, for 15–20 minutes. Season with salt and freshly ground pepper.

Remove the rump from the oven and stir the cooking juices into the gravy mixture. Place the meat directly onto a hot barbecue and cook for 20 minutes, browning all sides. For beef well done, cook a little longer. Remove from heat and leave to rest for 10 minutes before carving. Serve thinly sliced with the wild mushroom gravy. Serves 6–8.

Crackling roast pork with sage gravy

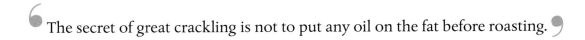 The secret of great crackling is not to put any oil on the fat before roasting.

2 kg boneless loin joint

salt

30 g butter, or bacon fat

1 clove garlic, chopped

½ onion, chopped

1 tablespoon fresh sage, chopped

1 beef stock cube

400 ml water

Preheat oven to 190°C. Wash the joint under cold water and put it on a roasting tray. Season with salt and put in the oven to roast for 2½ hours (25 minutes/ 0.5 kg plus 25 minutes).

To make the gravy, melt the fat in a frying pan and add the garlic, onion and sage. Cook for 3 minutes. Dissolve the stock cube into the water and add to the herb mixture. Bring to the boil and leave to simmer gently for 20 minutes.

Remove the pork from the oven and allow the juices to settle for 10 minutes. Remove the crackling from the top of the roast (the crackling can be put back into the oven if you want it to be even crispier). This makes carving a lot easier. Reheat the sage gravy. Put a few slices of meat onto each plate with a piece of crackling and a little gravy. Serves 6.

Murray's Aberdeen meatballs

'I cooked this dish before watching the Murray–Federer final at the U.S. Open in 2008. Federer won decisively 6–2, 7–5, 6–2 to win his 5th successive U.S. Open title, but Murray played really well (beating Nadal) to get there.'

Meatballs

2 kg lean Aberdeen minced beef

75 g white bread

water

2 eggs

1 tablespoon Worcestershire sauce

salt and pepper

50 g butter

Tomato Sauce

2 tablespoons olive oil

1 clove garlic, chopped

¼ onion, chopped

6 medium tomatoes, skinned and chopped

125 ml dry white wine

150 ml vegetable or chicken stock

½ teaspoon white sugar

2 tablespoons tomato purée

1 tablespoon chopped parsley

salt and pepper

Put the bread into a bowl and pour water over it until the bread is saturated. Leave for 5 minutes and squeeze as much water out of the bread as possible. Crack the eggs into a bowl and add the Worcestershire sauce. Whisk together using a fork. Combine the beef, eggs and bread together and season with salt and pepper. Mix well and roll into balls. Melt the butter in a frying pan and gently cook the meatballs until brown on all sides. Remove from heat.

To make the tomato sauce, melt the olive oil in a frying pan and cook the garlic and onion gently for 4 minutes. Add the tomatoes, white wine, stock, sugar and tomato purée. Simmer for 15 minutes and season with salt and pepper. Add the meatballs and fresh parsley and cook for a further 10 minutes. Serve with pasta and freshly grated Parmesan cheese. Serves 8–10.

Nadal's roast gammon

'We had a few friends around for lunch before the 2008 Men's Wimbledon Final. Both players played brilliantly. Seven hours and five sets later, and countless rain delays, Nadal finally defeated Federer 6–4, 6–4, 6–7, 6–7, 9–7 in what must have been the most exciting Wimbledon final ever. By the end of the match we had 16 people in our television room, and the gammon reappeared! This roast goes a long way. '

1 large gammon	3 tablespoons powdered mustard
3 tablespoons demerara sugar	8 cloves (optional)

Wash the gammon and put it into a large pot. Cover it with water and bring it to the boil. Empty the water and cover the gammon again with cold water. Return to heat and simmer for 3 hours (30 minutes per 0.5 kg plus 30 minutes), topping up the water as necessary. Drain and remove the rind, when cool enough to do so. Score the back gently with a sharp knife leaving incisions horizontally and vertically. Mix the powdered mustard and sugar together and sprinkle over the ham. Insert the cloves into each diamond shape. Place in a roasting dish and cook for 30 minutes at 210°C, or until golden brown.

Yoyo's herbs 'n' pork chops

'Yoyo Schepers, a great friend of mine from my Wimbledon days, taught me about cooking with herbs. The sage in this marinade deliciously complements the rich flavour of the pork.'

8 pork chops

3 tablespoons freshly chopped sage

2 tablespoons white wine

4 tablespoons olive oil

¼ teaspoon salt

¼ teaspoon freshly ground pepper

Wash the meat and pat dry. To make the marinade, combine the sage, wine, olive oil, salt and pepper and mix well. Roll the chops in the marinade, covering all sides. Cover, and leave to marinate in the fridge for at least three hours. Cook each side under the grill or on the barbecue for 8–9 minutes. Serve with mashed potatoes, petit pois and steamed carrots. Serves 8.

Bosham barbecue feast for 30

‘When the summer sun comes out in Sussex everyone wants to celebrate. What starts out as a small gathering soon doubles, then trebles and before you know it the numbers have swollen to thirty! On these occasions I provide the meat and drinks and everyone else brings a salad of their choice. ’

Menu: Barbecued Meat, Susie's Hot Potato Salad, Tamsin's Green Salad, and Juliet's Fruit Salad

Barbecued Meat
15 lamb chops
15 chicken pieces
30 spare ribs

Marinade
250 ml olive oil
1 clove garlic, crushed and chopped
5 tablespoons soy sauce
1 tablespoon brown sugar
1 teaspoon salt
5 tablespoons balsamic vinegar

Hot Potato Salad
1 kg new potatoes
2 red onions, chopped
8 shallots, chopped
5 boiled eggs, chopped
250 ml mayonnaise
2 tablespoons Dijon mustard
3 handfuls of fresh peas
1 teaspoon salt

Green Salad
10 Romaine lettuce hearts
5 medium lettuces
500 g cherry tomatoes
3 cucumbers
150 ml olive oil
90 ml white wine vinegar
1 garlic clove, chopped
20 leaves fresh basil, chopped
¼ teaspoon salt

Fruit Salad
1 pineapple
2 apples
3 mangoes
1 kg blueberries
500 g seedless grapes
4 punnets strawberries
juice of 1½ limes
rind of one lime
20 leaves fresh mint

Barbecued Meat

Wash and pat dry the meat and place in a bowl large enough to hold all of it. Make the marinade by mixing all the ingredients together and pour it over the meat. Roll the meat in the marinade ensuring that all sides are coated. Cover with cling film and leave in the fridge for at least three hours. Forty five minutes before serving, place the ribs on a rack and cook in a 190°C oven for 40 minutes. When the barbecue is hot, place the chicken pieces and the spare ribs on the grill and cook for 20 minutes. Place the lamb chops on the barbeque and cook for 15–18 minutes.

Susie's Hot Potato Salad

Wash the potatoes and place in a pot of salted water. Bring to the boil and cook the potatoes for 5–7 minutes. They should be cooked, but still firm. In a large serving bowl, combine the potatoes with the remaining ingredients and mix well. Serve while still hot.

Tamsin's Green Salad

Wash and dry the lettuce leaves. Put into a large salad bowl. Chop the tomatoes in half and slice the cucumbers, leaving the skin on. Roughly chop the basil leaves. Add the basil, tomatoes and cucumber pieces to the salad bowl. Make the dressing by mixing 150 ml olive oil with 90 ml white wine vinegar together with the garlic, salt and basil. Whisk the mixture with a fork. Pour the salad dressing on and toss just before serving.

Juliet's Fruit Salad

Cut the skin off of the pineapple and cut the flesh off of the core. Chop into 2 cm pieces and put into a large serving bowl. Core the apples and cut into 2 cm pieces. Peel the mangoes, remove the stones, and cut into 2 cm pieces. Clean the blueberries, cut the tops off the strawberries and chop in half. Cut the grapes in half. Add all the fruit to the fruit bowl. Pour the lime juice over the top, toss in the mint leaves and the lime rind and mix well.

Each to his choice, and I rejoice
The lot has fallen to me
In a fair ground – in a fair ground –
Yea, Sussex by the sea!

RUDYARD KIPLING
Sussex

Sizzling spare ribs

‘It is essential that pork be cooked thoroughly. I always err on the side of caution and cook my ribs in the oven first, then place them on the grill for a final sizzle. ’

3 kg spare ribs	2 teaspoons paprika
1 clove garlic, crushed	4 tablespoons white wine vinegar
2 teaspoons brown sugar	150 ml soy sauce
2 teaspoons mustard powder	2 tablespoons oil

In a medium sized mixing bowl combine the garlic, sugar, mustard powder, paprika, vinegar, soy sauce and oil. Roll the spare ribs around the sauce, covering completely. Allow the meat to marinate for at least an hour before cooking. Remove the ribs and place in a roasting pan. Save the leftover marinade. Cook in a moderate oven (160°C) for one hour before transferring to the barbecue. Cook for 7 minutes on each side, basting occasionally with the leftover marinade, until crispy brown. Serves 8.

Lewa Downs wildebeest stew

'The night before I ran a marathon in Kenya I was served a delicious wildebeest stew on an enormous bed of rice. I completed the race and, amazingly, was the fourth woman to cross the finishing line. I strongly recommend this rich protein/carbohydrate dish to any long distance runner – particularly when running in Africa!'

1.25 kg wildebeest meat, cut into 2 cm pieces

3 tablespoons oil

125 g back bacon

1 clove garlic, chopped

1 onion, chopped

2 carrots, roughly cut

2 stalks celery, chopped

1 tablespoon thyme

250 ml beef stock

125 ml red wine

1 bay leaf

8 black peppercorns

1 tablespoon juniper berries

1 tablespoon sugar

125 g button mushrooms

salt and pepper

2 tablespoons fresh coriander, chopped

Heat the oil in a large ovenproof casserole and braise the wildebeest meat for 3–4 minutes until all sides are brown. Remove with a slotted spoon and add the bacon, garlic and onion. Cook until the onions are soft and add the carrots, celery and thyme. Pour in the stock and the red wine and add the bay leaf, peppercorns, juniper berries, sugar and mushrooms. Season with salt and pepper. Return the meat to the casserole and place in a preheated 180°C oven for 2½ – 3 hours. Season with salt and pepper and garnish with fresh coriander. Serves 6.

A dog's meal

‘The golden rule when preparing fresh dog food is to use 75 per cent meat, 25 per cent vegetables. The meat can be either cooked or served raw. Crunchie and Willow find this dish, when cooked, irresistible. ’

500 g minced beef

125 g diced carrots, washed

3 teaspoons cod liver oil

2 teaspoons fresh parsley

Put all the ingredients into a large mixing bowl and mix until well blended. If your pet prefers their meal cooked, place in a frying pan and cook for 10 minutes. Remove from heat and cool. Divide into bowls and serve. Cats love this meal too – but in smaller quantities! Serves 2.

A woman should never be seen eating or drinking,
unless it be lobster salad and Champagne, the only
true feminine and becoming viands.

LORD BYRON

Fish
& Shellfish

Chichester Harbour lobster salad

'Lobster is delicious hot or cold and I prefer to have it hot in the evening and cold in the daytime. This is a very basic salad, but I don't fiddle too much with lobster – the meat is so delicious it needs little accompaniment.'

2 lobsters, boiled

250 g rocket lettuce

1 lemon, cut into wedges

freshly ground pepper

1 tablespoon chopped coriander

Wash and dry the rocket. Divide the lettuce and place onto four salad plates. Remove as much meat from the lobster shells as possible (I take my lobsters outside and cover a table with a sheet of plastic; then I set to work with a hammer, nutcracker and lobster pick). Once all the meat has been removed, arrange on top of the lettuce. Make a mayonnaise dressing (p.52) and put a large dollop on the side of each plate. Garnish with wedges of lemon, freshly ground pepper and chopped coriander. Serves 4.

Zigzag scallops

'Zigzag scallops are indigenous to Bermudian waters. They bed deep in the pink sands of the island's pristine beaches and are a delicacy second to none.'

500 g scallops

4 tomatoes

120 g butter

4 cloves garlic, crushed

1 medium onion, finely chopped

80 ml dry white wine

⅓ cup flat-leaf parsley, chopped

salt and pepper

fresh parsley, to garnish

Cover the tomatoes with hot water and leave for 5 minutes until the skins begin to come away from the flesh. Peel off the rest of the skin, remove the seeds, and chop into small pieces. Melt half the butter in a frying pan and cook the garlic and onion until soft, but not brown. Pour in the wine and add the tomatoes. Simmer for 5 minutes. Melt the remaining butter in another frying pan and cook the scallops gently for 4 minutes. Add the parsley and cook for 2 minutes more. Combine the scallops and the tomato sauce and season with salt and pepper. Serve in a shallow bowl, garnished with a little parsley. Serves 2–4.

Captain's House lobster

'I have eaten lobsters from all over the world and have learned that the colder the water, the better the lobster. This is not a dish for a formal evening – dig in and be prepared to get your hands wet!'

1 medium (1½ pound) lobster per person
60 g butter per person

¼ garlic clove per person, chopped
a pinch of salt per person

Bring a large pot of salted water to the boil. Immerse the lobster completely into the water, head first. Cover the pot and simmer for 15 minutes. Drain. Melt the butter and add the garlic and salt. Bring to the boil and remove from the heat. Using a hammer and a pair of scissors, crack the claws and cut the underside of the lobster from the base of the tail, through the legs, to within 2 cm of the head. There is a sac behind the lobster's eyes that you don't want to eat. Serve the lobster with melted garlic butter and white rolls.

Tito's calamari salad

'Josip Broz was the Yugoslavian revolutionary who came to be known as Tito (meaning "do this, do that"). His hideout was in a tiny cave high in the foothills of Vis, a spectacular island off the Dalmatian coast, and from there he led the resistance against the German invaders. The waters surrounding Vis are warm and clear and crawling with calamari.'

500 g young octopus meat

80 ml dry white wine

1 tablespoon flat-leaf parsley, chopped

1 tablespoon coriander, chopped

1 teaspoon fresh oregano, chopped

1 carrot, peeled and finely chopped

2 garlic cloves

80 ml olive oil

80 ml lemon juice

½ teaspoon salt

pepper

Wash the octopus under cold water and cut into one-inch pieces. Place the pieces into a pot, add the wine and enough water to cover. Bring to the boil and simmer for 45 minutes or until the meat is tender. Strain the calamari pieces and transfer to a serving bowl. Add all the other ingredients except the parsley and season with salt and pepper. Just before serving, toss in the parsley and serve with plenty of fresh bread. Serves 6.

Sam's skate wings

'Skate is best cooked quickly at a high temperature. Don't fuss over a sauce, it is so good on its own.'

4 skate wings

2 tablespoons olive oil

1 knob butter

salt and pepper

Wash and pat dry the skate wings. Heat the oil and melt the butter in a frying pan and cook the skate for 4–5 minutes on each side. Season with salt and pepper. Serves 4.

Sleeman's poached salmon

‘Scotland is renowned for its challenging fishing. Our great friend William is the only person I know who can catch a 13 lb salmon when the water level is low, the waves are white-capped and the wind is hurricane force. In fact, if there's a fish in there, he'll catch it!’

3 kg salmon
120 g butter
2 tablespoons oil
4 garlic cloves, crushed
1½ onions, sliced

300 g fresh greens, washed and sliced
salt and freshly ground pepper
1 teaspoon mixed herbs
3 bay leaves
1 lemon, finely sliced

Have your fishmonger clean and gut the salmon. Wash it under cold water and pat dry. Generously butter a large piece of foil and lay the fish on top, leaving about 5 inches on either end. Heat the oil in a saucepan and add the garlic and sliced onion. Add the greens and 60 g butter to the pot. Cover and cook gently for 3 minutes. Season with salt and pepper and a teaspoon of mixed herbs. Stuff the greens and onion mixture into the belly of the salmon. Sprinkle some salt and freshly ground black pepper over the back of the fish and lay the bay leaves and lemon slices across the top. Put 4 or 5 dabs of butter on top too. Fold the foil around the fish and make sure the fish is completely covered and no juices can escape. You may need to use an additional sheet of foil. Put the fish on a baking tray and place in a preheated 130°C oven for 3½ hours. Serve with boiled new potatoes, a green salad and Béarnaise sauce (p.49).

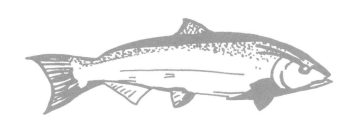

Fishbourne fish pie

'I have to find clever ways of getting my children to eat fish. This is one of them.'

900 g fresh local fish
400 ml whole milk
150 g butter
2 tablespoons plain flour
1 tablespoon olive oil
salt and pepper
2 tablespoons chopped tarragon

½ clove garlic, chopped
¼ onion, chopped
120 g prawns, peeled
1½ carrots, finely sliced
1½ leeks, finely sliced
3 eggs, hardboiled, peeled
900 g potatoes

Have your fishmonger skin and de-bone the fish. If you are doing it yourself, grab hold of the fish tail and using a sharp knife make an incision through the flesh near the tail to the skin but do not cut through it. Waggle the tail backwards and forwards until the flesh comes away from the skin. Wash the fish fillets under cold water and pat dry. Remove any remaining bones using tweezers. In a casserole dish, pour in 400 ml milk and lay the fish into it gently. Season with salt, pepper and a few dollops of butter. Cook in a preheated 200°C oven for 20 minutes. Remove the fish from the dish and set aside. Keep the milk stock. In a saucepan, melt 60 g butter and whisk in 2 tablespoons of flour. Gradually add half the milk stock, whisking continually. When all the milk has been integrated and the sauce has thickened, remove from heat. Pour one tablespoon of olive oil into a frying pan and cook the tarragon, garlic and onion for 3–4 minutes. Add the prawns, carrots and leeks and cook, covered, for 2–3 minutes. Return the fish and vegetables to the casserole dish and distribute evenly along the bottom. Slice the eggs and create a layer over the fish. Pour over the white sauce. Season with salt and pepper.

Peel the potatoes. Place them in a pot of cold water and bring them to the boil. When they are soft, mash them with 60 g butter, ¼ teaspoon of salt and 125 ml of milk stock. Create a top layer to the fish pie by spreading the mashed potatoes over the other ingredients. Crack a raw egg into a cup and whisk with a fork. Make slatted indentations in the potato using the fork and half the egg mixture. Place on the middle shelf of a 200°C oven for 30–40 minutes. Serves 6.

Severine's terrine de saumon

'We spent a lovely weekend in Brittany last summer visiting friends. The food in the French countryside is always delicious because the ingredients are fresh from the garden or local market.'

5 fillets organic salmon

30 g butter

5 eggs

125 ml crème fraîche

2 tablespoons mixed herbs

pinch of salt and pepper

3 tablespoons breadcrumbs

Preheat the oven to 200°C. Wash the salmon fillets and pat dry. Remove any bones. Heat the butter in a frying pan and gently cook the salmon. After 6 or 7 minutes remove from the heat. Combine the salmon together with eggs, crème fraîche, herbs, salt, pepper and breadcrumbs. Blend well (an electric mixer may be used). Place in a buttered terrine and cook for 40–45 minutes.

Skewered monkfish tails

I love monkfish because it has the same firm white flesh as lobster meat, which I adore. It is delicious hot or cold.

750 g monkfish tail	2 tablespoons olive oil
1 lemongrass stalk	½ tablespoon fresh basil, chopped
juice of 2 limes	1 lime, cut into wedges

Soak 4 wooden skewers in water for 20 minutes. Bash the lemongrass stalk and cut into fine strips. Add the lemongrass to the lime juice and olive oil. Cut the monkfish into one-inch pieces and pour over the lemongrass and lime juice marinade. Mix well, covering the monkfish all over. Marinate in the fridge until ready to cook. Thread the monkfish pieces onto the wooden skewers and grill for 4–5 minutes until cooked through. Garnish with chopped basil and a wedge of lime. Serves 4.

Grilled Dover sole

I used to be too afraid to cook Dover sole at home. It is expensive and I thought I might accidentally ruin it. This recipe is foolproof and I guarantee there will be no wastage!

6 whole Dover sole, trimmed	salt and pepper
150 g butter	1 lemon, cut into wedges
juice of 1 lemon	2 tablespoons fresh parsley, chopped

Wash the fish under cold running water and pat dry. Clarify the butter (melt it, let it separate and skim off the top fat). Pour the lemon juice over the fish and season with salt and pepper. Place the fish on a grilling rack and baste it all over with the clarified butter. Place under the grill and cook each side for 4–5 minutes. Serve with steamed green beans and boiled new potatoes. Garnish with lemon wedges and chopped parsley. Serves 6.

Moules marinières

'It is fun to use an empty mussel shell as pincers-cum-fork when eating. I also stack the empty mussel shells inside one another like Russian dolls. It saves space and helps to keep your plate tidy. '

2 kg live mussels

2 onions peeled, 1 chopped

3 peppercorns

¼ teaspoon salt

1 bay leaf

150 ml dry white wine

100 g butter

2 cloves garlic, chopped

1 tablespoon thyme, chopped

1 tablespoon flour

2 carrots, roughly cut

2 stalks celery, roughly cut

150 ml double cream

salt and pepper, to taste

1 tablespoon flat-leaf parsley, chopped

Wash the mussels under cold water and drain. Put the mussels into a large pot with the whole onion, peppercorns, salt, bay leaf, carrots, celery and wine. Cover with water and bring to the boil. Reduce the heat and simmer for 5 minutes. Remove the mussels from the pot and set aside. Strain the broth through a muslin cloth. Keep half the liquid and return it to the heat to simmer. Heat the butter and gently cook the garlic, thyme and chopped onions. Add the flour, stir, and remove from heat. Whisk the garlic and onions into the broth and simmer for 20 minutes. Stir in the cream. Season with salt and pepper. Return the mussels to the pot and reheat, but do not boil. Serve the mussels and broth in a bowl and garnish with chopped parsley. Serves 6.

Hemingway's tuna fish salad

'I once saw a tuna chasing a school of smaller fish in Croatia. It jumped five feet out of the water before disappearing back into the sea – an amazing sight.'

4 tuna steaks

8 tablespoons soy sauce

juice of ½ lemon

8 tablespoons olive oil

½ tablespoon freshly chopped ginger

1 clove garlic, chopped

black pepper

rocket lettuce, washed and dried

4 tablespoons fresh coriander, chopped

Wash the tuna under cold water and pat dry. Combine the soy sauce, lemon juice, olive oil, ginger, garlic and pepper in a bowl and mix well. Put the tuna steaks into the bowl and roll around in the marinade until completely covered. Leave in the marinade for at least one hour. Heat a grilling pan on the stove and put the tuna steaks on to sizzle for 3–4 minutes, depending on the thickness of the steaks. Flip the steaks over and cook for another 3–4 minutes. Serve on a bed of rocket and pour the leftover marinade over the top. Garnish with fresh coriander. Serves 4.

Then the fish came alive, with his death in him, and rose high out of the water showing all his great length and width and all his power and his beauty. He seemed to hang in the air above the old man in the skiff. Then he fell into the water with a crash that sent spray over the old man and all over the skiff.

ERNEST HEMINGWAY
The Old Man and the Sea

Golden cod cakes

'Coriander and cod are a marvellous marriage of flavours. This recipe is very popular at home, even among the non-fish lovers. '

1 kg cod fillets, skinned and de-boned
150 g butter
800 g potatoes, peeled
4 tablespoons cream
3 tablespoons parsley, chopped
5 tablespoons coriander, chopped

salt and pepper
seasoned plain white flour, for coating
4 tablespoons olive oil
4 tablespoons sour cream
1 lemon, cut into wedges

Melt 60 g butter in a frying pan and gently cook the cod until it is white and flaky. Remove from heat and place on a warm plate. Quarter the potatoes and boil in a pot of salted water for 15 minutes or until soft. Thoroughly mash the potatoes with the remaining butter and cream and season with salt and pepper. Add the fish, parsley and 3 tablespoons chopped coriander. Mix well. Divide into 8–10 equal portions and dip into the seasoned flour, coating all sides. Heat the oil (medium-high temperature) in a frying pan and fry the cakes for 4 minutes on each side, until they are golden brown. Serve with a dollop of sour cream and garnish generously with the remaining coriander and a wedge of lemon. Serves 8–10.

Tennyson's seafood melée

'Alfred Tennyson visited Bosham in 1865 and wrote of the idyllic life the fishermen seemed to lead in this quaint seaside village. Although few of the coastal cottages are occupied by fishermen today, their appearance hasn't altered much and they retain all of their original character. This soupy spaghetti dish is excellent served after a day spent on the water or at the beach, when the fresh air and salt water are still fresh in one's memory, if not still on one's skin!'

200 g smoked back bacon
1 tablespoon cooking oil
1 onion, diced
2 tablespoons flour
3 leeks, finely cut
250 g mushrooms, sliced
120 g butter
1 chicken stock cube

250 g fillets lemon sole, skinned and de-boned
400 g shrimp
440 g scallops
250 ml whole milk
2 tablespoons freshly chopped dill
400 g spaghetti
salt and freshly ground black pepper

Fry the bacon in a little oil until the pieces are beginning to brown on each side. Remove from the pan and leave to cool on some kitchen paper. Pour the fat from the bacon away, but do not rinse the pan. Gently fry the onions in the bacon fat residue until they are soft. Add the leeks, mushrooms and 30 g butter and crumble a stock cube over the top. Mix in and cook for 8–10 minutes. Chop the fat off the bacon and cut the meat into medium-sized pieces. Add the pieces to the pan along with the sole, shrimp and scallops. Fry on medium heat for 8 minutes. Season with salt and freshly ground black pepper. Remove from heat and cover. Bring a pot of water to the boil, add a little salt and cook the spaghetti as per instructions on the packet (roughly 10 minutes). When it is ready, drain. Meanwhile, melt the remaining butter in a small pot and stir in the flour. Gradually add the milk and whisk continually until the sauce is smooth, hot and beginning to thicken. Combine the fish and vegetables together with the white sauce and pour over the pasta. Garnish with fresh dill. Serves 6.

Line caught buttered cod

'This is a simple but delicious recipe. The hard part is catching the fish. '

4 fillets of cod

1 tablespoon olive oil

100 g butter

2 garlic cloves, chopped

salt, to taste

1 tablespoon fresh parsley, chopped

Wash the fish fillets under cold water and pat dry. Heat the olive oil in a frying pan and add the butter. Lightly fry the garlic for 1 minute and lay the fillets into the pan. Cook on medium heat for 4–5 minutes, depending on the thickness of the fillets. Remove from heat, season with salt and fresh parsley. Serves 4.

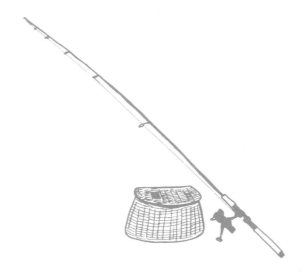

There is no sincerer love than the love of food.

GEORGE BERNARD SHAW

Vegetables

Millstream vegetable kebabs

'These kebabs get ten out of ten for presentation! Serve alongside any grilled meat or fish dish.'

5 tablespoons olive oil	juice of 1 lemon
3 tablespoons soy sauce	1 red pepper
¼ red chilli, chopped	1 green pepper
1 clove garlic, crushed and chopped	1 yellow pepper
1 teaspoon chopped thyme	3 medium courgettes
1 teaspoon chopped tarragon	1 aubergine

Make a marinade by mixing together the olive oil, soy sauce, chilli, garlic, herbs and lemon juice. Wash and de-seed the peppers. Cut them into 3 cm cubes. Wash the courgettes and the aubergine, chop the ends off and slice finely. Soak the vegetables in the marinade for 20 minutes. Soak 4 wooden skewers in water for 20 minutes. Thread the vegetables onto the skewers and cook on a hot barbecue or under a grill until the vegetables start to brown at the edges. Serves 4.

Stuffed marrow roast

After Charlie and I were married I had to learn how to cook all of his favourite dishes. This was one of them.

1 marrow (1 foot long)
2 tablespoons olive oil
1 clove garlic, crushed
½ onion, chopped
1 kg lean minced steak

1 tablespoon Worcestershire sauce
1 tablespoon parsley
1 beef stock cube
4 tablespoons grated Parmesan cheese

Wash the marrow and slice it in half. Scrape out the inner pith and seeds and rest on a rack in a baking tray. Heat the oil in a frying pan and cook the garlic and onion. Add the lean mince, Worcestershire sauce and parsley. Crumble the stock cube with your fingers, sprinkle over the meat, and mix in. Fill the marrow halves with the meat and pour 80 ml water into each half marrow. Fill the bottom of the baking tray with 2–3 cm water, but do not let the water touch the marrow. Cover with foil and cook in a preheated 180°C oven for 1 hour. Remove the foil and sprinkle the grated Parmesan on top. Turn the oven up to 200°C. Put the stuffed marrow back into the oven and cook, uncovered, for another 15 minutes. Serve with Béchamel sauce (p.47). Serves 6.

E. M. F. H

This is our family code for "each man for himself". After a large lunch when no one is quite hungry enough for an evening meal (especially me), we each help ourselves to whatever is left in the larder. Believe it or not, it is a family favourite!

Trippet tart

'This is one of the simplest dishes to make. It makes a delicious light lunch and there are never any leftovers. It is even more delicious if you are eating outside, on the Trippet, watching the tide coming in. '

375 g puff pastry

4 eggs

40 ml whole milk

300 g green beans

½ red pepper

1 tablespoon olive oil

2 pieces back bacon

40 g Parmesan shavings

salt and pepper

Roll out the puff pastry and line a baking dish. Whisk the eggs together and brush the edges of the pastry with it. Pour the milk into the eggs and mix well. Season with salt and pepper. Wash and trim the green beans and the slice the pepper. Steam them for 2–3 minutes until they are cooked al dente. Fry the bacon in the olive oil, remove the fat and cut into small pieces. Place the beans, pepper and bacon pieces on top of the pastry and pour in the egg mixture. Scatter the Parmesan shavings over the top and place into a preheated 190°C oven for 25 minutes. Serve with a green salad.

Steamed Finlaystone artichokes

'Barbara was the first friend I made when we moved to Sussex five years ago. Sadly, the MacMillans have moved back to Finlaystone, the family's home in Scotland. There they have a wonderful house and garden and when they came to visit us this summer they brought the most magnificent globe artichokes I have ever seen.'

12 globe artichokes
750 g butter

4 garlic cloves, chopped
½ teaspoon salt

Shorten the stems of the artichokes to about ½ cm. Soak in a large pot of salted water for half an hour. This rids the artichokes of insects and dirt. Trim off the rough outer leaves using a knife or a pair of kitchen scissors. Bring a large steamer to the boil and put the artichokes in. Season with salt and pepper and steam for 35–45 minutes.

Melt the butter in a saucepan and add the garlic and salt. Remove the artichokes from the pot and place each one on a plate. Serve with a side dish of garlic butter. Serves 12.

William the Conqueror's green bean salad

'I make a large bowl of this salad as it keeps for 2 or 3 days if refrigerated. Summertime is extremely busy in our household, and it is handy to have a salad always available. '

1.5 kg French beans
2 tablespoons olive oil
200 g back bacon
1 clove garlic, chopped
125 ml olive oil

50 ml white wine vinegar
¼ teaspoon salt
freshly milled black pepper
200 g Parmesan cheese, roughly cut

Put the beans in a steamer and cook for 3–4 minutes until cooked but still firm. Run under the cold tap to prevent further cooking. Drain and set aside. Place the oil in a frying pan and cook the bacon until both sides are starting to brown. Remove the fat and cut into pieces. Set aside on a sheet of kitchen towel. To make the dressing, crush the garlic and mix with the olive oil, vinegar, salt and a little freshly milled black pepper. Place the green beans, Parmesan and bacon into a serving dish. Pour the dressing over the top and mix well. Serves a crowd.

Bosham Bell peppers

'There is a legend that a band of Norse pirates came to Bosham and pillaged the church, stealing the great tenor bell. When the villagers discovered that their main bell was missing, they rang the remaining bells, causing the great tenor bell to break loose from the longboat to which it was bound, and sink to the bottom of Bosham Channel. Today, when the church bells ring, the one at Bell Hole at the mouth of the estuary still joins in. Try these grilled peppers on a Thursday evening (practice night for the Holy Trinity Bosham Bellringers) and see if you can hear the answering note . . . '

1 tablespoon olive oil

1 clove garlic, crushed and chopped

¼ onion, chopped

1 yellow pepper, diced

3 dried tomatoes, chopped

1 chicken stock cube

330 ml boiling water

100 g couscous

30 g butter

2 large red peppers

1 tablespoon fresh basil, chopped

2 x 30 g soft goat's cheese slices

salt and pepper, to taste

Heat the oil in a frying pan and gently cook the garlic and onions until soft. Add the yellow pepper and the dried tomatoes and cook for 2 minutes. Season with salt and pepper. Dissolve the stock cube in the boiling water and pour over the couscous. Add a little butter to the couscous, stir in, and cover for 5 minutes. Cut the red peppers in half and remove the seeds. Combine the cooked yellow pepper and tomato mixture with the couscous and fresh basil and stuff into the red peppers. Cover with a slice of goat's cheese and mill a little fresh black pepper over the top. Place under the grill for 5–7 minutes until the cheese has melted and is golden brown. Serves 4.

Roast Sussex tomatoes with couscous and chèvre chaud

'Sussex tomatoes are sweet and flavourful. This dish makes a splendid light summer meal.'

150 g couscous	3 tablespoons sour cream
500 g spinach	100 g goat's cheese, sliced
1 chicken stock cube	pinch of ground nutmeg
500 ml boiling water	freshly ground pepper
6 slices prosciutto	2 tablespoons fresh basil, chopped
4 large ripe plum tomatoes, sliced	

Grease a casserole dish and pour in the dried couscous. Wash the spinach and add to the casserole. Crumble a stock cube over the spinach and pour the boiling water over the top. Cut the prosciutto into 2 cm pieces and scatter over the spinach. Next add a layer of sliced tomatoes. Dollop on the sour cream and the goat's cheese and season with a pinch of nutmeg and some freshly ground pepper. Place in a preheated 200°C oven for 15 minutes until the cheese has melted and is golden brown. Remove from the oven and garnish with fresh basil. Serve with a green bean salad (p.131). Serves 4.

Native corn on the cob

‘This is how I imagine the North American Indians cooked their corn. This corn is delicious with lots of butter melted on top. ’

6 ears corn

120 g butter

salt, to taste

Bring a large pot of water to the boil and completely immerse the corn. Leave to boil for 5–7 minutes. Remove the corn from the pot and once it is cool enough to handle, peel the sheaf back from the cob, remove all the fine hairs, and leave the sheaves attached at the stem. Place on a grill over a fire (or in a preheated 200°C oven) for 5–10 minutes until the sheaves dry out and start to brown. Cover in butter and season with a pinch of salt. Eat with your hands. Serves 6.

Valda's chanterelles with onions and sour cream

❛The best place to find chanterelles on Meisner's Island is on the northern tip, underneath the pine trees. Every year, without fail, they are there. This is my mother's recipe.❜

600 g chanterelles
1 large onion
75 g butter, for frying

350 ml sour cream
salt and pepper

Chop the chanterelles and onion into small pieces. Add a little salt and fry separately until all the water has evaporated from the mushrooms. When the onions are soft and beginning to brown, add to the mushroom pan and mix in. Just before serving, add the sour cream but do not let it boil, as it will curdle. Season with salt and pepper. Serve on toast. Serves 4.

Jans' roasted vegetables

' I know summer is here when I have roasted vegetables on a bed of couscous in front of me. This is a light, colourful dish and is perfect for a picnic. '

1 red pepper	2 carrots
1 green pepper	1 clove garlic, chopped
1 yellow pepper	3 tablespoons olive oil
½ aubergine	½ teaspoon salt
2 courgettes	

Preheat the oven to 200°C. Chop the peppers, aubergine and courgettes into 2 cm pieces. Peel the carrots and slice them in half lengthwise. Chop coarsely. Put all the vegetables into a casserole or roasting tin and sprinkle the chopped garlic over the top. Pour over the olive oil and salt. Mix well, and roast in the oven for 10–15 minutes. These vegetables can be served hot or cold.

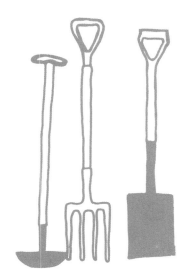

Mamma Mia's Greek salad

Feta cheese is the national cheese of Greece and has been produced in the mountainous areas of the country for over six thousand years. It can be served on its own with *psomi* (bread) or as a side salad. Either way it makes me sing!

5 cucumbers	2 tablespoons chopped fresh basil
5 tomatoes	200 ml olive oil
½ onion, optional	100 ml white wine vinegar
100 g pitted black olives	salt
300 g feta cheese	freshly ground black pepper

Wash the cucumbers and cut them lengthwise, then across, making bite sized cubes. Next wash and cut the tomatoes, making similar sized pieces. Slice the onion into quarters and then proceed to cut roughly. Put the cucumbers, tomatoes and onion into a serving bowl and add the olives, feta and chopped basil. Make the dressing by combining the vinegar and olive oil and adding a pinch of salt. Toss into the salad and garnish with black pepper. Serves a crowd.

Marrow delight

Parmesan is the finest and most readily available of the Italian cheeses. This recipe is very basic, but the Parmesan transforms the courgettes into a tasty delight.

5 courgettes	a pinch of salt
4 tablespoons grated Parmesan cheese	

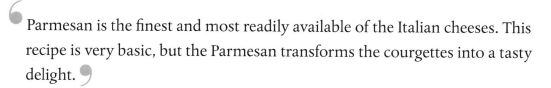

Preheat the oven to 220°C. Wash and cut the ends off the courgettes. Slice each lengthwise, twice, creating four strips. Place the strips in an ovenproof dish and sprinkle with a little salt. Put in the oven and cook for 10 minutes. Remove and cover with Parmesan cheese. Return to the oven and cook for a further 8 minutes. Serve immediately.

Everything you see I owe to spaghetti.
SOPHIA LOREN
Italian actress

Egg
& Italian

Champion omelette

'The television set is rarely off during the Wimbledon fortnight in most English households and it is no different at Creek House. For lunch, just before the Serena versus Venus final, I served this omelette with a Greek salad and a loaf of homemade bread. Venus played brilliantly, after a slow start, and it was a great victory for her. Her demure smiles during the post match interview were endearing and showed us just what a great champion she is.'

11 eggs
250 ml whole milk
a pinch of salt
2 tablespoons olive oil

250 g Leicester cheese, grated
1 tablespoon grated Parmesan cheese
salt and pepper

Preheat the oven to 200°C. Whisk the eggs, milk and salt together in a mixing bowl. Rub the olive oil all around the inside of a large baking dish and pour the mixture in. Place the grated cheese on top of the eggs and season with salt and pepper. Place on the middle rack of the oven for 10–15 minutes until the omelette has risen and the top is golden brown. Serve with a little grated Parmesan on top. Serves 6.

Italian tomato and mozzarella salad

❝Everything about this dish reminds me of Italy: the smell, the flavour – even the colours are those of the flag.❞

600 g mozzarella cheese

5 large, ripe plum tomatoes

10 leaves fresh basil

50 ml olive oil

salt and pepper

Slice the mozzarella and tomatoes. On an attractive white serving dish (so as not to upset the colour scheme) alternate the tomatoes and mozzarella slices. Scatter the basil over the top and drizzle with olive oil. Season with salt and freshly ground pepper.

Mature cheddar cheese soufflé

'I was so proud of my first soufflé. I called the whole family in to the kitchen to watch as I took it out of the oven. It was tall and light and surprisingly easy to make!'

50 g butter	½ teaspoon cayenne
25 g flour	4 egg yolks
250 ml milk	5 egg whites
150 g mature cheddar cheese	salt and pepper
½ teaspoon dry mustard powder	

Preheat the oven to 190°C. Tie a collar around the soufflé dish and fasten it with a piece of string. Butter the inside of the dish. Melt the butter in a saucepan and stir in the flour. Gradually whisk in the milk until it is well integrated and smooth. Reduce the heat, and cook slowly for another 3 minutes, stirring continually. Remove from heat and stir in the cheese, mustard powder and cayenne. Season with salt and pepper. Beat the egg yolks together using a fork and stir into the sauce, a little at a time.

Put the egg whites into an electric mixer and beat until quite stiff. It is essential not to over-beat the whites as the air bubbles 'pop' and the soufflé will not rise quite so high. Stir one tablespoon of the beaten egg whites into the yolk mixture, before carefully folding in the rest. Transfer to a straight-sided soufflé dish and put on the middle shelf of the oven. Cook for 20 minutes until the soufflé has risen and is golden brown. Serve immediately. Serves 4.

Cajun lasagne

'Every once in a while I like a really hot dish. This lasagne will blow you away!'

8 sheets lasagne

2 tablespoons olive oil

1 onion, chopped

2 cloves garlic, chopped

1 tablespoon oregano

1 tablespoon thyme

1 teaspoon salt

¼ teaspoon powdered hot mustard

1 tablespoon paprika

1 tablespoon cayenne pepper

1 kg lean steak mince

2 x 400 g tin chopped tomatoes in tomato juice

1 teaspoon granulated sugar

salt and pepper

80 g Parmesan cheese

2 teaspoons crushed chillies

325 g mozzarella cheese, cut into cubes

White sauce

600 ml whole milk

60 g butter

50 g plain flour

Boil the lasagne noodles as per the instructions on the package. Remove from water and mix in a little oil to prevent sticking. Set aside. Heat a little oil in a large frying pan and cook the garlic and onion for 1 minute. Add the oregano, thyme, salt, mustard, paprika and cayenne. Stir the steak mince into the herbs and spices and cook until the meat is brown. Add the tomatoes and sugar and bring to the boil. Cook for 5 minutes and season with salt and pepper.

To make the white sauce, melt the butter in a saucepan and stir in the flour. Gradually add the milk, whisking continually, until the milk is well integrated. Remove from the heat.

Preheat the oven to 180°C. Grease the inside of a casserole dish and pour 100 ml of white sauce in followed by 3 or 4 lasagne sheets, some meat sauce, Parmesan and one third of the mozzarella cheese. Repeat the process until all the sauces are in neat layers. Put one final layer of mozzarella and Parmesan on top and sprinkle with crushed chillies. Place on the middle shelf of the oven for 30 minutes. Serves 6–8.

Fettuccine carbonara

"I have picked up a few gardening tips from my friend Melissa over the years and one of them was to plant herbs in tubs just outside one's back door. It is very convenient having them close by, and one can send children out to do the cutting without too much protest. This creamy Italian dish can be easily prepared when there is very little in the larder. Just grab a handful of fresh herbs and you're all set."

Sauce

250 g back bacon

½ tablespoon olive oil

1 garlic clove, chopped

¼ onion, chopped

1 tablespoon fresh thyme, chopped

1 tablespoon fresh marjoram, chopped

1 tablespoon fresh sage, chopped

500 ml crème fraîche

salt and pepper

Pasta

500 g fettuccine pasta

1 tablespoon olive oil

¼ teaspoon salt

Cut the fat off the bacon and cut into 2 cm pieces. Heat the oil and fry the bacon in a large frying pan. Remove the bacon from the pan and replace with the garlic and onion. Cook for one minute. Add the thyme, marjoram and sage and cook for another minute before adding the crème fraîche. Reduce heat and let simmer for 15–20 minutes. Season with salt and pepper.

Boil a large pot of water and add ¼ teaspoon of salt and 1 tablespoon olive oil. Cook the pasta as per the guidelines on the packet. Drain and place in a large serving bowl. Pour the cream sauce over the pasta, add the bacon and stir. Serves 4.

Potatoes, pickles and pecorino

'The strong, salty flavour of the pecorino cheese adds a rich Italian flavour to this divine potato salad. '

20 medium sized potatoes

3 Haimisha cucumbers (dill pickles)

2 spring onions

2 tablespoons flat-leaf parsley, chopped

80 ml olive oil

2 teaspoons chopped fresh thyme

1 teaspoon lemon juice

1 clove garlic, crushed

¼ teaspoon salt

1 teaspoon ground black pepper

20 g pecorino cheese

Wash and cut the potatoes, but do not peel. Put them in a pot of salted water and bring to the boil. Cook for 5–7 minutes until the potatoes are still firm, but cooked through. Rinse under cold water and drain. Slice the pickles and chop the spring onions. Mix one tablespoon parsley, oil, thyme, lemon juice, and garlic together in a cup using a fork. Place the potatoes onto a large serving dish and add the pickles and onions, salt and pepper. Pour the dressing over the potato salad and mix well. Garnish with grated pecorino and the remaining parsley. Serves 8–10.

Pasta 'n' frankfurters

‘This is my daughter Katie's recipe. She wears swimming goggles while chopping the onion!’

750 g pasta

2 tablespoons olive oil

1 green pepper, diced

6 rashers back bacon, chopped

1 onion, finely chopped

6 frankfurters, chopped

7 mushrooms, sliced

1 tablespoon parsley, chopped

1 tablespoon basil, chopped

400 g tomato sauce

Boil the water and put the pasta in. Cook for 8–10 minutes. In a frying pan, pour in the olive oil and add the diced pepper, bacon, onion, basil, parsley, frankfurters and mushrooms. Cook for 5 minutes on medium heat and then add the tomato sauce. Bring to the boil. Drain the pasta when it is cooked. Put the pasta onto a plate and pour the sauce on top. Serves 6.

Tattie 'n' ratatouille

'Ratatouille is one of the most versatile dishes I know. It goes well with fish, pasta, chicken, and jacket potatoes. Even on its own with a slice of homemade brown bread it is an immensely satisfying meal.'

1 red pepper	2 cloves garlic
1 green pepper	5 tablespoons olive oil
1 yellow pepper	1 tablespoon coriander seeds
1 onion	salt and pepper, to taste
1 courgette	4 jacket potatoes, baked
1 aubergine	2 teaspoons freshly chopped coriander
4 medium tomatoes	

Chop the peppers, onion, courgette, aubergine and tomatoes into 2 cm pieces and keep in separate piles. Peel the garlic cloves and chop into tiny pieces. Pour 3 tablespoons of oil into a frying pan and over medium heat add the garlic and onions. After one minute add the peppers. Add a little bit more oil to the pan and add the courgettes and aubergines. Bring to the boil and let simmer for about 20 minutes. Add the coriander seeds and the tomatoes and season with salt and pepper. Cover and simmer for 20 more minutes. Serve with a jacket potato and garnish the ratatouille with freshly chopped coriander. Serves 4.

Lunchtime margharita pizza

❝Pizza is a lunchtime dish. If my children had their way, we would have lunch three times a day.❞

Dough
1 teaspoon yeast
450 g white flour
1 teaspoon salt
250 ml water
2 tablespoons olive oil

Topping
250 g mozzarella cheese
8 leaves fresh basil

Sauce
2 tablespoons olive oil
1 clove garlic, chopped
2 teaspoons fresh oregano
2 x 400 g tins chopped tomatoes in
    tomato juice
1 teaspoon sugar
pinch of salt
black pepper

Using a bread machine, put the yeast into the bread pan, followed by the flour, salt, water and olive oil. Start the PIZZA/BAKE program. When the program has finished, remove from the pan and place on a floured work surface. Knead the dough until it is smooth and elastic. Sprinkle a little more flour onto the counter top and roll the dough into a large circle. Grease a pizza pan and place the pizza dough onto it. Cover with cling film and leave in a warm corner of the kitchen until ready to use.

Heat the oil in a frying pan and add the chopped garlic and oregano. Pour in the tomatoes and sugar and simmer for 20 minutes. Season with salt and pepper.

Preheat the oven to 200°C. Remove the cling film from the pizza base and spread the tomato sauce on top. Sprinkle with a teaspoon of olive oil. Cut the mozzarella into pieces and scatter over the top of the pizza along with the basil. Put in the middle of the oven and cook for 15 minutes or until the cheese is golden brown. Makes two large pizzas.

Summer time an' the living is easy,
Fish are jumpin' an' the cotton is high.
Oh, yo' daddy's rich, and yo' ma is good-lookin',
So hush, little baby, don' yo' cry.

DU BOSE HEYWARD
'Summertime',
from *Porgy and Bess*

Puddings
& Beverages

London Granny's Christmas pudding

'My father's mother was generous of spirit and very theatrical. I can just imagine her making this cake. Step aside Galloping Gourmet!'

230 g stale bread

230 g margarine

230 g currants

230 g raisins

230 g sultanas

115 g ginger preserve

115 g mixed candied peel

115 g chopped almonds or cashew nuts

6 eggs

½ teaspoon nutmeg, grated

½ teaspoon powdered cinnamon

½ teaspoon powdered cardamon

½ teaspoon powdered cloves

1 teaspoon salt

1 wine glass (125 ml) brandy

1 wine glass sherry

1 wine glass rosewater

1 or 2 tablespoons sugar (optional)

Break the stale bread into pieces and mix together with all the other ingredients. Steam in a sealed container for 2 hours. Turn onto a tray. Heat the brandy, pour over the pudding and set on fire. Serve with brandy butter (butter, icing sugar and brandy).

Aunt Gilly's love cake

'This recipe is a legacy of the Portuguese who once ruled the island of Ceylon. It is chewy and sweet and is always served at happy occasions.'

500 g chopped cashew nuts
250 g butter
625 g sugar
12 egg yolks
6 egg whites
250 g pumpkin preserve
250 g semolina (very fine)

1 dessertspoon vanilla essence
½ dessertspoon rose essence
2 dessertspoons honey
2 dessertspoons brandy
½ dessertspoon powdered cinnamon
rind of 1 lime or lemon
pinch of salt

Combine the sugar and egg yolks together and beat for 15 minutes. Heat a frying pan and lightly roast the semolina. Mix in the butter and add to the sugar mixture. Beat for 5 minutes. Add the cashew nuts and pumpkin preserve and beat for 3 minutes. Mix in the essences, honey, brandy, cinnamon and lemon rind. Beat 6 egg whites with a pinch of salt until they are stiff. Fold into the cake mixture. Line a baking tray with 4 sheets of newspaper and one sheet of greaseproof paper and carefully pour in the mixture. Bake on the middle shelf of a 150°C oven for half an hour. Reduce to 120°C and cook for another half hour. Leave to cool and cut into small pieces.

Chidmere apple pie

'In September, the Bosham foreshore is littered with apples from Chidham. They float across the estuary, coming in with the tide. When I see them on the beach, I am reminded that it is apple pie time and I beg a bag of apples from my friends, the Russells, who live at Chidmere House. This pie is delicious served with warm custard or a scoop of vanilla ice cream.'

Pastry
300 g plain white flour
2 tablespoons icing sugar
1 teaspoon baking powder
¼ teaspoon salt
190 g butter
1 egg
4–5 tablespoons cold water
½ teaspoon vanilla extract

Filling
700 g cooking apples, peeled and cored
juice of 1 lemon
3 tablespoons brown sugar
½ teaspoon cinnamon
¼ teaspoon ground nutmeg
¼ teaspoon ground cloves
40 g butter, divided into 5 cubes

Topping
1 egg, beaten and 1 tablespoon caster sugar

To make the pastry, sieve the flour, icing sugar, baking powder and salt together into a large mixing bowl. If you have an electric mixer, combine the butter and the flour combination until a breadcrumb-like mixture forms. Otherwise, quickly integrate the butter into the flour mixture using your fingertips. Make a well in the centre and crack an egg into it. Gradually mix in the water and vanilla with a round bladed knife until the pastry mixture comes together. Wrap in cling film and leave to rest in the fridge for 25–30 minutes. Once chilled, remove the pastry from the fridge and roll out onto a flat, floured surface. Lightly grease an 11-inch pie dish. Lay the pie dish upside down on the flattened dough and cut 1 inch around the dish. Create another circle with the leftover pastry. Flip the dish over and line it with the larger pastry circle. Cut the apples into large chunks and roll them in lemon juice to prevent browning. Place the apple pieces in the pastry shell and drizzle them with the leftover lemon juice. Sprinkle with brown sugar, cinnamon, nutmeg and ground cloves and dot with cubes of butter. Cover the pie with the remaining pastry. With your fingertips, press the top and bottom pastry circles together, using a little beaten egg to bind them, if necessary. Tidy the edges and use any leftover pastry to decorate the pie. Finally, make a small hole in the middle of the pie for the steam to escape and place in a preheated 200°C oven for 40–50 minutes. Remove from the oven, brush with a little beaten egg and sprinkle with caster sugar. Return to the oven for 3–5 minutes or until the top is shiny and golden brown. Serves 8–10.

Coffee chocolate brownies

'My husband says these are the best brownies he has ever had. Be warned, however, they are incredibly rich.'

Brownies

120 g butter

120 g unsweetened milk chocolate

60 g sweetened milk chocolate

60 g plain flour

180 g granulated sugar

2 eggs, beaten

1 teaspoon vanilla extract

1 tablespoon instant coffee

180 g chopped macadamia nuts (optional)

Icing

25 g margarine

50 g icing sugar

1 teaspoon cocoa powder

Preheat oven to 180°C. Butter a 6 x 9 inch baking dish. Melt the butter and the unsweetened chocolate together in a double boiler and set aside. Sift together the flour and sugar. Make a well in the centre and add the eggs, vanilla and coffee. Mix well. Add the melted chocolate and stir until all ingredients are well integrated. Break the sweetened milk chocolate into pieces and stir into the mixture. Add the macadamia nuts. Transfer to the baking dish and place in the centre of the oven for 20 minutes. Remove from the oven and leave to cool in the baking dish for 10 minutes before transferring to a wire rack.

To make the icing, mix the icing sugar, margarine and cocoa powder together with a few drops of water. Spread the icing over the top of the brownies once they have cooled. Makes 15 brownies.

Eton Mess

Eton Mess is traditionally served at the school's prize giving each year. I doubt they include the liqueur in their recipe, but mine certainly calls for it. Add a little extra and really make a mess of it! Raspberries can be substituted if you miss the strawberry season.

Meringue
4 egg whites
200 g caster sugar

Mess
800 g fresh strawberries
125 ml fruit liqueur
2 tablespoons icing sugar
175 ml double cream
175 ml Greek yoghurt

Beat the egg whites (make sure there is absolutely no egg yolk present) in an electric mixer on medium speed for one minute. Gradually increase the speed until soft peaks begin to form. Add the sugar, a little at a time, until it is completely integrated. Spread onto a sheet of parchment paper and put in a preheated 140°C oven for one hour. Turn off the heat entirely and leave in the oven for 3 hours. Break the meringue into small pieces once it has cooled.

To make the Mess, cut the tops off the strawberries and cut into quarters. Soak ¾ of the strawberries in 100 ml liqueur and sift half the icing sugar over the top. Purée the remaining icing sugar, strawberries and liqueur in a blender. Whip the cream until it begins to thicken and fold in the Greek yoghurt. Leave the strawberries, fruit purée and yoghurt mixture in the fridge to chill.

When ready to eat, gently stir the strawberries, yoghurt mixture and meringue until a neat swirl effect has been created. Pour the strawberry purée over the top and serve immediately.

This road
floods
each tide

T

PLANT REGROWTH
MONITORING
AREA

Muddy Bosham chocolate mousse

'Bosham mud is a rich, thick, gooey composite and I love it – much like this pudding.'

250 g plain milk chocolate

6 egg yolks, beaten

2 teaspoons vanilla essence

400 ml double cream

30 g white chocolate

Melt the milk chocolate over a double boiler. Whisk together the egg yolks and the vanilla essence and combine with the chocolate. Whip the cream until thick and fold in the chocolate mixture. Place into 4 serving bowls and leave to set in the fridge for 2 hours. Grate a little white chocolate over the top to garnish. Serves 4.

Old fashioned coffee vanilla ice cream

‘I like to make ice cream the old fashioned way. We were given an ice cream maker years ago for Christmas but the box has never been opened!’

3 tablespoons instant coffee

65 ml hot water

2 eggs

150 g caster sugar

500 ml double cream

185 ml milk

2 teaspoons vanilla essence

Dissolve the coffee into the hot water and cool. Whisk the eggs together for two minutes and very slowly add the sugar. Combine the coffee, milk and vanilla essence and stir into the egg mixture. Whip the cream until it is thick, but not too stiff, then carefully fold in the coffee mixture. Pour into a Tupperware container (fill an appropriately sized one) and leave in the fridge to chill for 2 hours. Cover and transfer to the freezer. When the mixture is half frozen, remove from the freezer and beat for one minute. Return to the freezer. Serves 6.

Willow's tarte au citron

'This is our English Setter's favourite pudding. Once we caught her standing on the kitchen table finishing off the last piece. '

Pastry:
200 g plain flour, sifted
a pinch of salt
100 g butter
3 tablespoons iced water
4 tablespoons flour for rolling out

Filling:
3 eggs, beaten
160 g caster sugar
juice of 6 lemons
zest of 1 lemon, very finely grated
90 ml double cream

Garnish
crème fraîche
fresh mint

To make the pastry, combine the flour and salt in a bowl. Add the butter and use your fingertips to rub the butter into the flour until the mixture resembles breadcrumbs. Measure 3 tablespoons of iced water and pour over the flour mixture. Work the water into the dough using a round-bladed knife until a ball of pastry is formed. Roll the pastry out onto a floured, cold surface. Line a tart dish with the pastry and cook in a preheated 200°C oven for 10 minutes. Reduce the heat to 130°C and leave the pastry to brown for a further 20 minutes.

To make the filling, preheat the oven to 190°C. Whisk together the eggs and sugar. Stir in the lemon juice and lemon zest. Add the cream and mix slowly until well integrated. Pour the mixture into the pastry shell and bake for 40 minutes until the filling has a custard-like consistency. Remove from the oven and sprinkle with a little icing sugar. Serve warm with a dollop of crème fraîche and a sprig of fresh mint on top.

Significant birthday cake with irresistible icing

'There are two things to remember if one is to create a light and moist cake: first, sift the flour and second, cream the butter and sugar until it resembles whipped cream. I always let my children ice the cake as they do the best job – no matter what the age or the formality of occasion. They decorate it with sweeties of their own choosing, which makes the cake all the more irresistible. '

Cake	Icing
550 g butter	60 g butter, room temperature
550 g granulated sugar	750 g icing sugar
550 g plain white flour, sifted	3 tablespoons vanilla extract
1¼ teaspoons salt	90 ml milk
10 teaspoons baking powder	½ cup cocoa
700 ml milk	sweets of your choice
5 teaspoons vanilla essence	
10 egg whites (medium eggs)	

Preheat the oven to 200°C. Cream the butter and gradually add the sugar. Sift the flour, salt and baking powder together and stir into the butter mixture. Pour in the milk and vanilla and whisk into the batter until all the lumps have disappeared and the batter is smooth. Beat the egg whites (make sure there is no trace of yolk) until stiff peaks form. Carefully fold into the batter and transfer to two 12-inch buttered and floured baking tins. Put on the middle shelf of the oven and cook for 55–60 minutes, or until the cakes 'bounce back' and a knife comes out clean. Remove the cakes from the oven and transfer to a wire rack to cool.

To make the icing, cream the butter, sugar and vanilla and add the milk and cocoa, alternately, until the mixture has the consistency of a smooth paste. Once the cakes are cool, stack them and cover entirely with the icing. Decorate with lots of sweeties. Serves 12–15.

Alexa's Eyes

'My likoo eye beginning with 'd'
ditch, donkey, dustbin? – *'No No'*
drain, Daddy, dog, duster. Diaper? – *'Oh No'*
It's a nappy – Stop correcting me so!

As we motor along on the road to the coast
Alexa and Sam strapped in tight,
Mummy and Daddy are looking around
for the 'd' that Alexa caught sight.

Inside and out, on the road, in the air
we scour for new 'd's as we drive
but at every guess we are greeted with *'No!'*
from our little one with her bright eyes.

After minds have gone blank, not a glimmer of hope
we give up and await the great word
for she surely has seen something that we have not
something small perhaps, maybe a bird?

'Birthday Cake!', cries Alexa; we should really have guessed,
same as g, c, k, y, p and a
for Alexa sees birthday cakes in every shape
she continues to see them today.

For an artist can see what mere mortals cannot
it explains why we all love them so
and Alexa remains the best of the lot
the definite star of the show.

Ed's chocolate-covered strawberries

'My daughter's friend, Ed, has *the* knack for dipping strawberries!'

225 g plain (good quality) chocolate

3 tablespoons double cream

1 teaspoon prepared coffee

1 punnet dry strawberries, room temperature

Put the chocolate into a small pot and melt it over a pan of hot water. Add the cream and coffee and stir until evenly integrated. Hold the strawberries, one at a time, by the stem and dip halfway into the melted chocolate. Dry upside down on a rack or on a piece of parchment, or simply pop it straight into your mouth!

Clafouti aux poires

Laetitia, my daughter's friend, made this pudding for us when we visited her family in Brittany. It is a perfect dish to serve at breakfast, as it is basically a custard and fruit recipe. In Brittany, we ate it at tea, which is also a good time to have it.

375 g sweet pastry

5 fresh pears, peeled and de-seeded

6 eggs

200 g caster sugar

300 ml crème fraîche

1 teaspoon vanilla essence

2 tablespoons dark brown sugar

Preheat the oven to 200°C. Separate 4 eggs and whisk the egg whites until thick. Beat the leftover yolks and remaining 2 eggs and stir in the sugar. Combine the crème fraîche and vanilla with the egg and sugar mixture. Fold in the egg whites. Roll out the pastry on a floured work surface and place carefully into a buttered pie dish. Slice the pears and arrange the pieces on top of the pastry and pour in the batter. Sprinkle a little brown sugar over the top and place in the middle of the oven. After 10 minutes reduce the heat to 190°C and cook for another 25–30 minutes. Serves 8.

Manor House Cavalier cake

'Legend has it that under the old stones of the Bosham Manor are Cavalier jewels and buried cash. Although much restoration has recently been done to the house, no hidden treasures have yet been unearthed. Perhaps they are buried deep within the elusive tunnel which allegedly links the Manor House to the ancient Saxon church. If you are entertaining children, why not wrap a few coins in foil and slip them into the batter before baking? With or without hidden treasure, this cake is my teatime favourite.'

150 g butter	1 dessertspoon baking soda
150 g caster sugar	½ unwaxed lemon peel, grated
4 eggs	½ unwaxed lime peel, grated
200 g flour	1 teaspoon vanilla essence
pinch of salt	2 tablespoons icing sugar

Cream the butter and sugar together in an electric mixer. Beat the eggs and slowly add them to the butter and sugar. Mix in the vanilla essence. Sift the flour, salt and baking soda together. Remove the bowl from the electric mixer and fold the dry ingredients into the egg mixture. Add the lemon and lime peel. Mix well. Transfer mixture to a greased baking tin and put in the centre of a 180°C oven for 50 minutes, or until golden brown. Place on a wire rack to cool. Sift a little icing sugar over the top before serving.

Chester blueberry crumble

6 The Ondaatjes hit Meisner's Island like a storm every summer. That's about twenty-five mouths to feed, three times a day. Fortunately, this crumble recipe can be doubled, halved, or trebled to whatever one's requirements may be. 9

500 g flour   2½ kg blueberries
250 g butter   50 ml water
150 g brown sugar

Mix the flour and butter together in an electric mixer until the mixture resembles breadcrumbs. Add the sugar and mix well, but be careful not to overdo it. Clean the blueberries and pour into a large casserole dish. Pour the water in with the blueberries and sprinkle the crumble mixture over the top. Place in a preheated 180°C oven for 40 minutes or until the topping is golden brown. Reduce the heat to 140°C and cook for another 20 minutes. Serves 12.

Parham summer pudding

'Nestled between the South Downs and Storrington lies Parham House, where James and Lady Emma Barnard and their family live. Last summer we had the most delightful evening there. The atmosphere at Parham, with its fabulous historic fireplaces and collection of Elizabethan paintings, and the buzz of excited children dashing in and out of the drawing room created a magical evening. This summer pudding will make your mouth sing!'

1 kg summer berries (blueberries, raspberries, blackcurrants and redcurrants)
50 ml Crème de Cassis

150 g caster sugar
10 thick slices good quality white bread
whipped cream

Clean the fruit and put into a pot with the Cassis and sugar. Bring to the boil and let simmer for 4 minutes. Remove from the heat. Butter a 16 cm pudding basin and line the bottom and edges with the bread, making sure not to leave any gaps. Gently firm the bread into place and pour the fruit and juices into the bowl. Cover the bowl with the last few slices of bread and place a flat plate on top, and on top of that another 1 kg weight. Place the pudding into the fridge and leave for 10 hours. Serve with lightly whipped, slightly sweetened whipped cream.

Chocolate ice cream elixir

❝Chocolate contains health-promoting substances called flavonoids. Thank heavens!❞

100 g plain chocolate	185 ml milk
65 ml water	500 ml double cream
2 eggs	150 g caster sugar
2 teaspoons vanilla essence	

Place the chocolate and water into a saucepan and melt the contents over a double boiler. Whisk the eggs together until light and fluffy. Pour the vanilla and milk in with the eggs and mix well. Whip the cream until it is quite thick, but not too stiff, and gradually blend in the sugar. Fold the egg mixture carefully into the whipped cream. Finally, fold in the melted chocolate. Pour into an appropriately sized Tupperware container and leave in the fridge until thoroughly chilled. Cover the container and transfer to the freezer until the mixture is half frozen. Remove from the freezer and beat for one minute. Return to the freezer. Serves 6.

Moorish chocolate chip cookies

'These are the best chocolate chip cookies I have ever come across. You'll find it hard to stop at just one . . . '

250 g butter

200 g brown sugar

200 g granulated sugar

2 eggs

1 tablespoon hot water

2 teaspoons vanilla

200 g flour

1 teaspoon salt

1 teaspoon baking soda

300 g chocolate chips

Preheat oven to 190°C. Cream together the butter, brown sugar and granulated sugar in a large bowl. Add the eggs, hot water and vanilla and beat until fluffy. Sift together the flour, salt and baking soda and stir into the egg mixture. Pour in the chocolate chips and mix well. Using a teaspoon, evenly place drops of cookie dough onto a well-buttered baking sheet. Flatten lightly using a wet fork. Place on the middle shelf of the oven and bake for 8–10 minutes. The cookies should be puffy in the centre and lightly brown at the edges. Remove from the oven and cool on a wire rack. Any unused dough can be frozen. Makes 24.

Old Park sugar pie

'Our friends the Alun-Jones host an annual cricket game at their house, Old Park, every summer. It is a huge amount of fun and Deborah and Jeremy always throw a bash – a party for the teenagers and dinner for the adults – after the match. This year, the evening was warm and we were able to dine by candlelight out on the terrace. This sugary, yet creamy pie was absolutely delicious and I managed to get Debs to divulge her recipe.'

pastry of your choice
½ teaspoon baking soda
¼ teaspoon vanilla extract
375 ml maple syrup
145 g plain white flour

150 g dark brown sugar
pinch of nutmeg
80 g butter
125 g pecans

Roll out the pastry on a floured surface and line a 9-inch pie dish. Stir the baking soda and vanilla into the maple syrup and pour into the pastry shell. Sprinkle the pecans on top of the maple syrup. Combine the flour, sugar, nutmeg and butter together using your fingertips until the mixture resembles breadcrumbs, and then spread over the pecans. Place the dish onto a baking sheet lined with foil (to catch the overflow) and bake at 190°C for 30 minutes. Allow to cool before serving. It is best cold.

Inedible playdough

'The secret here is to add so much salt and food colouring that no child will ever be tempted to eat it!'

200 g plain white flour

200 g salt

2½ tablespoons cream of tartar

325 ml water

3 tablespoons sunflower oil

food colouring

Sift together all the dry ingredients in a mixing bowl. Whisk together the water and oil and blend into the flour mixture. Place in a pot and cook gently until a smooth ball of dough forms. This should take about 5 minutes. Remove from the heat and knead in the food colouring. Store in an airtight container or a plastic bag until playtime.

Alexa's ginger beer

'It's hard not to get involved in the spirit of brewing something new in our house. When we heard that my husband's company was coming out with a delicious new ginger beer, my daughter quickly exclaimed, "I know how to make ginger beer. We made it in chemistry class!" Here is her recipe. It is quite delicious.'

1 lemon

2 tablespoons grated ginger root

230 g white granulated sugar

¼ teaspoon cream of tartar

¼ teaspoon dried yeast

2 litres hot water

Grate the lemon peel and ginger root. Put the lemon rind, ginger root, sugar, cream of tartar and yeast into a large screw-top plastic bottle and pour in the hot water. Squeeze the lemon and pour the juice into the bottle. Stir the bottle gently until the sugar dissolves. Store in a warm place for 24–48 hours. Serve chilled.

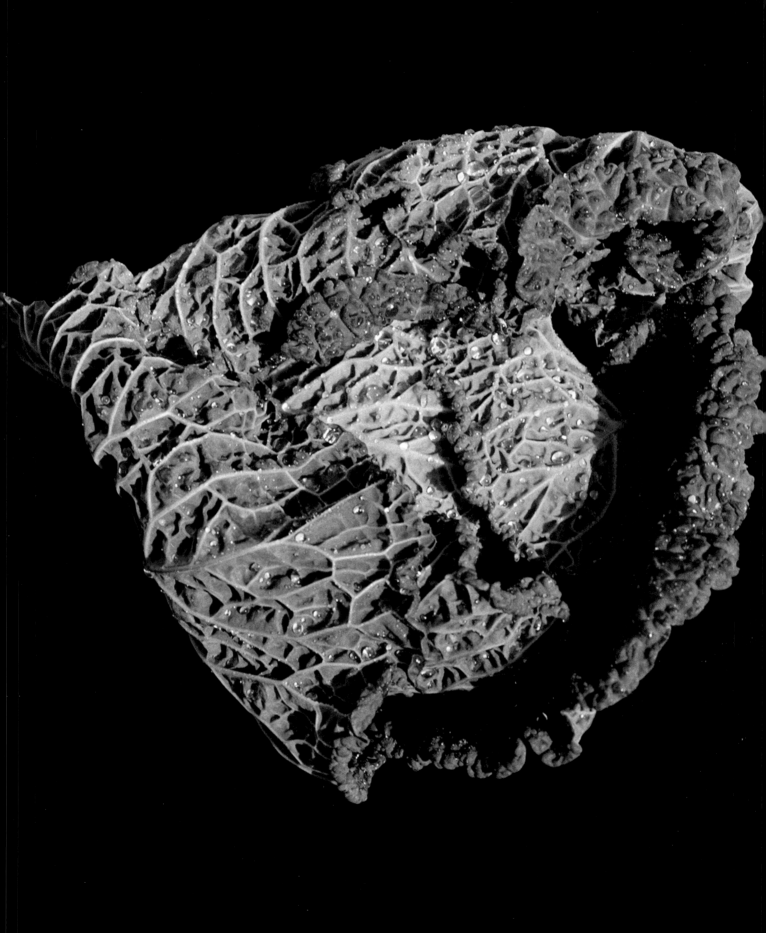

Seasoning chart

	beef	chicken	fish	lamb	curries	pork	cheese	vegetables	eggs	tomatoes	cakes
allspice											O
aniseed			O		O						O
basil							O		O	O	
bay	O	O	O	O	O	O					
black pepper	O	O	O	O	O	O	O	O	O	O	
caraway							O				O
cardamon					O						O
cloves					O	O					O
coriander	O	O	O	O	O	O	O	O			
cumin					O	O		O			
dill			O				O		O	O	O
fenugreek					O						
fines herbes		O	O	O		O	O	O	O	O	
garlic	O	O	O	O	O	O	O	O	O	O	
ginger			O		O	O					O
juniper		O				O					
mace			O								O
marjoram	O	O	O	O	O		O	O		O	
myrtle	O	O	O	O		O					
nutmeg		O						O			O
oregano	O	O	O	O			O	O	O	O	
parsley	O	O	O	O	O		O	O	O	O	
rosemary	O	O	O	O		O		O	O	O	
saffron			O	O	O		O		O		O
sage		O	O	O			O		O		
tarragon	O	O	O					O	O	O	
thyme	O	O	O	O			O	O	O	O	
tumeric					O				O		
vanilla											O

Index